WESTMINSTER SCHOOLS

SMYTHE GAMBRELL
LIBRARY

Alex Brissette

PRESENTED BY

Luke Allison
1992

SAVE THE EARTH
An Action Handbook for Kids

SAVE

An Action

THE EARTH

Handbook for Kids

by BETTY MILES

with drawings by Nelle Davis

and photographs

 ALFRED A. KNOPF   NEW YORK

THIS IS A BORZOI BOOK PUBLISHED BY ALFRED A. KNOPF, INC.

Book design by Mina Greenstein
Manufactured in the United States of America
10 9 8 7 6 5 4 3 2 1

Library of Congress Cataloging-in-Publication Data
Miles, Betty. Save the earth : an action handbook for kids / by Betty Miles ; illustrated with drawings by Nelle Davis and with photographs.—Rev. ed.   p.   cm.
Rev. and updated ed. of: Save the earth. Includes bibliographical references and index. Summary: An overview of the environmental problems of land, atmosphere, water, energy, plants, animals, and people. Includes projects and a section on becoming an environmental activist.
ISBN 0-679-81731-X (trade)   ISBN 0-679-91731-4 (lib. bdg.)
1. Pollution—Juvenile literature. 2. Environmental protection—Juvenile literature.
3. Pollution—Experiments—Juvenile literature. [1. Pollution. 2. Environmental protection.] I. Davis, Nelle, ill. II. Miles, Betty. Save the earth. III. Title.
TD176.M55 1991 363.7—dc20 90-46514

ACKNOWLEDGMENTS

As I've worked on this book, I've had help from many people. I'm grateful for the kindness, interest and enthusiasm of each one of them. They've shown me directly what thinking globally and acting locally means as they go about saving the earth, one step at a time.

I'd like to thank:

Lee Abrahamson, Chester Brigham, George Brigham, Anna Brown, Nick Byrne, Trieu Duong, Erwin Fleissner, Tom Furrer, Barbara Fussiner, Matty Goodman, Jason Grace, Jay Holcomb, Andrew Holleman, Marguerite Holloway, Naomi Hood, Rich Karkoska, Joseph Kiefer, Sharon Kinsman, Dory Kistner-Morris, Martha Kronholm, Ita Leach, April Lehman, Kate Malmrose, Norbert Rivera, Rosa Rivera, Gale Soltish, Mary Sprague, Carolyn Thorne-Lyman, Benny Vasquez and Denise Whitehead.

Special thanks to Ellen Miles, for research and for writing the Check It Out section; to Matt Miles, for thoughtful help at every stage of the manuscript; to Janet Schulman, for suggesting and supporting this book; to Mina Greenstein, for spirited design; to Susan Kassirer, for sensitive copyediting; to Maureen Sullivan, for diligent photo research; to Ruth Katcher, for her dedication, competence and care in bringing this book to completion; and above all to Frances Foster, my editor and friend.

A lot of people think kids can't do very much work in the world. But I think kids might be the only chance.

—ANNA BROWN, 11

Contents

Introduction

Humankind has not woven the web of life. We
are but one thread within it. Whatever we do to
the web we do to ourselves. All things are bound
together. All things connect. Whatever befalls the
earth befalls also the children of the earth.
　　　　—SEALTH (1786–1866)
　　　　　Chief of the Squamish and Allied Tribes

ALL people on earth share one home: our bright, fragile planet,
circling the sun in the vast blue darkness of space.

All living things on earth—the uncountable varieties of plants and
animals and human beings that grow and reproduce themselves and
die—depend on the earth's environment to sustain them. They are—
we are—part of the great web of life that has existed for millions of
years, and will keep on existing for as long as the earth can support
it.

The earth is always changing. Storms and fires, winds and droughts,
earthquakes and floods and the slow, strong force of water over rock
change the land and seas and the climate around them. Over long
periods of time these natural changes have affected all life on earth.

Today people are changing the earth faster and more drastically
than any force of nature. There are so many of us—more than five
billion now, and thousands more being born every hour. Each one of
these human beings needs food and shelter and security. But we haven't
yet learned how to manage the earth's resources so that everyone can
have these basic things. We are using up the earth's resources, like
clean air and fresh water, before we have learned to distribute them
fairly among all people. We are damaging the earth's environment
before we have learned how to restore it. We are changing the earth
in ways that may never be undone.

But we are also learning to save it.

Around the world, people are becoming aware of the urgent need
to stop destroying the environment and start restoring it—now, before it is too late. In the United Nations and in individual countries,
in political parties, in large organizations and in small community
groups, people are beginning to understand the connections between
their own needs and wants and the health of the whole planet. They

are marching, protesting, working and finding others to work with them. They are learning how to save the earth.

You can join them.

Think Globally, Act Locally

The earth's grave problems, like overflowing landfills, oil spills and acid rain, are huge and discouraging. Sometimes these problems seem impossible for ordinary people to solve. You may wonder what you can do.

People who work for the environment have a saying that may be helpful to you as you use this book: *Think globally, act locally.*

Thinking globally means being aware of the earth's big problems—understanding that they're connected, that they're influenced by forces like politics and population and poverty, and that no matter where they occur, they can affect everyone on earth.

Thinking globally is like looking at a whole forest and seeing beyond the beauty of the trees. It means thinking about the forest's history, its wildlife, the resources it provides, the people it supports. When you think globally, you think about the forest's effect on the climate around it, about over-logging, acid rain and soil erosion. You think about world-wide action to preserve forests and provide jobs for people who depend on them for a living. That's taking a global view.

When you start thinking globally, it's easier to see how *acting locally* fits in. Acting locally is planting one small tree, and caring for it, and then planting another one. It's getting a friend to plant a tree, too—maybe getting everyone in your town to plant trees. Acting locally means doing what you can, where you are, to help the environment.

Thinking globally, acting locally, we can save the earth—starting right now.

LAND

For billions of years the land on earth was wild, unspoiled, with space enough and food enough for all the people who lived on it.

Now billions of people live on the land and more people are born each day to share its limited resources. The amount of productive land on earth is steadily growing smaller. Farm land wears out from over-use, coastal land erodes, forest land is slashed and burned.

Cities grow and spread over the land around them. People who can no longer make a living on the land come to the cities in search of jobs. The cities keep growing. Poor families crowd together in slums or in shantytowns on the cities' fringes, and the cities expand without plan or design.

Suburban sprawl.

By the year 2000, the world's population will exceed six billion.

In some places this unplanned sprawl takes over, and formerly green suburbs turn into new cities, with urban problems of traffic and over-building. Open land is paved over and people are cut off from the countryside. Instead of growing their own food or buying it from nearby farms, people must buy food that has been grown far away and trucked for long distances.

Cities in developed countries create enormous amounts of trash every day. (In developing countries, there is simply less to throw away, and people save and reuse whatever they can.) Every piece of trash has to go somewhere. Whether it is dumped nearby or trucked to distant landfills, most trash will lie on the land for decades, releasing toxic chemicals and metals into the soil. These poisons threaten the health of the people living or working near landfills. If the toxins leach into the water supply they can endanger large populations hundreds of miles away.

Chemical plants, power plants, coal mines and factories also pollute the land around them with toxic wastes. Nuclear waste from power plants and arms factories is the most long lasting of all. Whether it is stored above the ground or buried deep beneath it, today's nuclear waste will be deadly to life on earth for thousands of years to come.

Damaged forest land.

Land contaminated by toxic waste.

In some parts of the world, like Eastern Europe, the land is so polluted by a mix of industrial poisons that no crops can be grown there safely. In most countries, chemical fertilizers and pesticides used on crops deposit poisons on the land that will infect future plant growth.

Farm land is being destroyed—sometimes irreversibly—in other ways as well. Planting the same crop for many seasons uses up the nutrients in the soil. Over-planting—never allowing the land to rest—will eventually make the land useless for farming. Irrigation harms the land when too much water floods the soil, rotting the roots of plants and letting the rich topsoil blow away. When dry lands are over-watered, salts left on the soil's surface as the water evaporates make it unfit for growing crops.

Cutting down the earth's old-growth forests destroys thousands of acres of land each day. This destruction may never be reversed. The soil on land that is stripped of its trees easily blows away. Even if new trees are planted, they cannot reproduce the conditions of a forest that has matured over time through cycles of growth, where towering trees are part of a complex ecosystem that cleans the air, traps flood waters and supports a great variety of wildlife.

In too many parts of the world, land is destroyed by the wars that rage over it. People cannot build homes or plant crops when their land is ruined by warfare and when they fear for their lives.

Land, to most of us, means more than just the ground beneath our feet. It means the place where we live: a special landscape, a community, a country—our home. But many people live on land that is

War in El Salvador.

damaged or barren and unable to sustain them. Many others have had to leave their homelands to look for work in cities, where they are cut off from any real connection with the open countryside. Millions of people on earth today have no place to call their home.

Saving the Land

The earth's land is divided into nations, but the problems are international. One country's trash can be exported and dumped on another country's land. Crops grown in one country's poisoned soil can be sold in many other countries. These problems demand international solutions, and the nations of the world are beginning to seek them together. Nations are also working together to preserve the earth's last wild places, recognizing that wilderness everywhere is part of the heritage of all peoples.

While cities continue to grow, there are planners in all of them who understand people's needs for trees and parks and easy access to unspoiled countryside. City governments are creating bike and hiking trails, requiring builders to provide parks around office buildings and developments and supporting the use of empty lots for community gardens where families can grow their own flowers and vegetables.

Careful planning can preserve open land.

 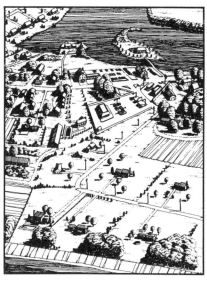 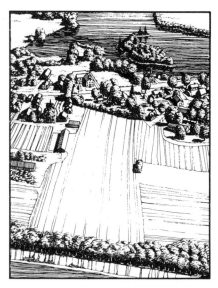

A village before development, surrounded by fields and woods.

An unplanned development, where houses and lots cover all the land.

A planned development, where houses are grouped to preserve open land.

People have begun to realize that when we throw something away it ends up *somewhere,* most likely in a landfill, where it can remain for decades. We're realizing that we've run out of space on the land for our trash, and that we must learn to make less of it. This means buy-

A landfill.

ing less to start with, and keeping what we have and using it longer. It means lending and sharing things we own and giving things we don't need to people who can use them. It means, above all, recycling—and people *are* recycling, in their homes and in their towns.

When laws against polluters are enforced, companies are less likely to poison the land with industrial wastes. An organization called Citizens Clearinghouse for Hazardous Waste is helping thousands of local citizen groups fight polluters. The organization was founded by Lois Gibbs, whose own neighborhood in Love Canal, New York, was declared a disaster area after years of contamination by a chemical company. Her family and hundreds of others had to be evacuated from their homes. Today Lois Gibbs helps others fight back.

Many groups, like the Children's Rainforest, are working to preserve forests around the world. Meanwhile, every tree we plant in our own communities helps to preserve and beautify the land.

Around the world, people are urging governments to support farm policies that will reduce the use of toxic fertilizers and pesticides and encourage farmers to use natural methods of pest control and soil enrichment, improving the land for future generations instead of wearing it out during our own lifetime.

In every country people are working for peace, so that all citizens of earth can feel safe on the land where they live.

■ The United States has three million miles of paved roadway. Roads and parking lots take up 10 percent of the land that is suitable for farming.

■ A plastic beverage container by the side of the road will have a longer life than the person who threw it there.

■ There are more than 58 million square miles of land on earth—nearly one-third of the earth's surface.

■ Forests cover 31 percent of the land, about 25 percent is pasture or rangeland, and 11 percent is planted with crops. This productive land is shrinking in size. The remaining 33 percent is either wasteland or land that is paved over or built on; this land is expanding.

■ Twenty-four billion tons of agricultural topsoil wash or blow away each year.

■ It's estimated that the earth is losing 14 million tons of grain each year from damage to the land and to crops.

■ Every ton of recycled paper saves approximately 17 trees, in addition to savings in dumping costs and landfill space.

■ Out of every $11 we spend for groceries, $1 goes for packaging. One-third of the weight of waste in town landfills comes from packaging.

■ Only 34 of the 1,175 most dangerous toxic waste dumps in the United States have been cleaned up since 1980, when Congress established the Superfund to pay for the work. It is estimated that 30,000 more toxic dumps will need to be cleaned up in the future.

■ In 1990, the United States recycled about 10 percent of its trash. Japan recycled about 50 percent.

■ Every man, woman and child in the United States produces an average of four pounds of garbage per day.

■ Andrew Holleman vs. the Developer

Andrew Holleman loves the woods near his home in Chelmsford, Massachusetts. He grew up exploring them, learning about the great blue herons, the deer, wood turtles, salamanders, mountain laurel and lady's slippers he found there.

But when Andrew was twelve, his parents got a letter saying that a developer was planning to build a 180-unit condominium complex on sixteen acres of the woods—almost half of them wetlands. There would be a hearing about it at the town hall.

"I was just plain angry that 'my land' was going to be destroyed," Andrew says. "I had to do something."

Andrew Holleman.

What he did first was head for the library, where he studied the state law that protects wetlands and his own town's master plan, which called only a small part of the land developable.

Next, he wrote a petition against the development and took it around his neighborhood, asking everyone to come to the hearing. Fifty other families whose land touched the property were notified about the hearing by the developer. Because of Andrew's efforts, more than 250 people attended.

After the developer spoke, Andrew stood up and showed a wood turtle shell he had found in the woods. He explained that a condominium development would destroy the habitat of some rare plants and animals. He suggested another site—an old drive-in movie lot—where the developer could build without such destruction.

That was only the beginning. Next, Andrew wrote letters to state representatives and senators and to his local TV station. He called the "Helpline" at the Massachusetts Audubon Society, where a biologist suggested ways to fight the development. Andrew and his father helped to form a neighborhood association to stop the condo project.

It was a long fight. The developer took his case to commissions and to appeal boards. For seven months, there were meetings every week, some more than three hours long and many of them on school nights. People said that Andrew should give up, that the developer would surely win in the end. But Andrew wouldn't give up.

The developer's last hope was to pass a series of deep-hole tests for drainage, to see if a deeply dug hole on the site would fill up with water and prove the land a bad place to build. Many people came to the woods to watch the test. Andrew was sure the site would fail the test. It did.

Nine months after the developer first announced his plans, the town of Chelmsford denied permission to him, or to anyone else, to build a large development on the site. Now the developer is building his condos on the old drive-in site that Andrew had suggested. The woods are safe—at least for now. And Andrew is working to get the state to buy the land, so it will remain wild forever.

■ The Toxic Avengers of *El Puente*

The Toxic Avengers are a group of young people who live in Brooklyn, New York, and meet at *El Puente,* a neighborhood center. They're fighting toxic waste. They're also fighting what they call "environmental racism"—allowing factories that pollute to exist in poor and minority neighborhoods.

The founding members of the group discovered pollution in their

Toxic Avengers at a waste site.

own neighborhood as part of a class project. With their teacher, José Morales, they took samples of waste from a street gutter near the vacant lot where a local factory kept chemical waste in barrels. Their laboratory analysis showed the samples to be toxic and flammable. They then learned that a local warehouse stored hazardous and radioactive waste. They wondered: do polluters think that in a Hispanic neighborhood, people won't care?

The Toxic Avengers of *El Puente* set out to show that people *do* care. They began to challenge the polluters. When they organized a demonstration against the hazardous-waste warehouse, community leaders and citizens of all ages turned out to demonstrate with them. The Avengers intend to keep up the pressure until they get the warehouse out of their neighborhood.

The Avengers believe that too many major environmental groups ignore what's going on in poor and minority communities. They don't know of another group like theirs—but they don't let that stop them. They don't let the fact that they're not adults stop them from speaking out and organizing.

The Toxic Avengers think young people in other neighborhoods should be aware of environmental issues that affect them.

"Know what you're doing," says member Rosa Rivera, "and don't be intimidated by adults who try to put you down. By working together, you can really make a difference."

Redesign Your Town

An Ongoing Project

Most people would like their towns to be different—to have more open space, or less traffic, or more good places to sit and talk.

Most towns have zoning codes that determine how the land will be allocated for business, homes and public use. Town planning boards make changes as needs change. Sometimes the changes are good for the environment and sometimes they're not.

Here's a way to see how your town's environment could be improved:

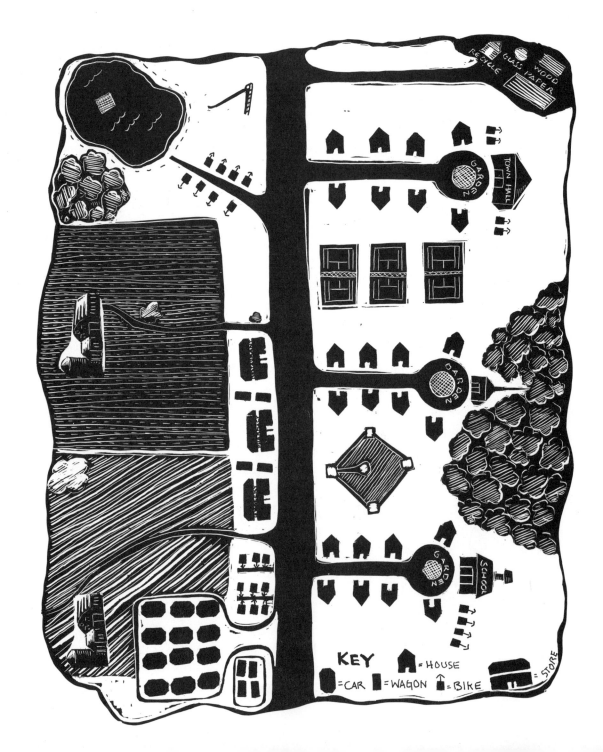

Get a zoning map from your town hall or library. Make several copies.

Draw the outlines of the map on tracing paper.

On Map 1, draw your town as you would like it to be, without worrying about its current zoning. Here are some things to keep in mind:

> trails for biking and walking
> low-traffic streets
> easy walking to shops and schools
> places to sit outdoors
> parks and woodlands
> recycling centers
> community gardens
> safety for young children
> recreation for all ages
> access for the physically disabled and elderly

On another outline map, make changes in your town's current zoning to achieve as much of your Map 1 wishes as possible. Call this Map 2.

Make as many maps as you need in order to come up with a realistic, environmentally sound zoning plan for your town.

Now that you know more about the process of planning, you can understand some of the problems your own town's planning board faces.

Most planning boards hold open meetings. If you've done this project with a group like a school class or a scout group, you might want to attend a meeting together and share your ideas.

Human Garbage Can

A One-Week Project

Want to see how much trash one person (you, for example) throws away in a week? Students at Dartmouth College did this project to find out.

Get yourself a garbage bag—a big, strong one.

Every time you have something to throw away—scrap paper, plastic bottles, soda cans, food scraps, tissues, cartons, magazines, paper plates, juice cartons, food containers, glass jars, paper bags, plastic bags, *everything*—put it in this bag.

Fasten the bag tightly.

Carry the bag with you wherever you go.

At the end of the week, you will know how much trash one person can make.

If you do this experiment with a group of people, you could have a public weigh-in at the end of the week. Put all the trash together and see how much you've collected. If you sort out the recyclable trash

into a separate pile you'll see very clearly how recycling can reduce landfills.

This is a dramatic project. When you finish you might want to call a press conference or make a videotape.

☐ When you go shopping, bring along a string bag or a used shopping bag. Every paper or plastic bag you use twice saves one bag.

☐ Don't buy over-wrapped products, like individually wrapped cheese slices. That unnecessary plastic will sit in landfills for hundreds of years.

☐ Don't use a plastic bag to hold produce like celery, cucumbers, melons or anything else you can easily put in a shopping cart.

☐ Choose frozen juice concentrate instead of juice in cartons or jugs, to reduce packaging.

☐ Don't be fooled by plastic products labeled "biodegradable." They *will* break down into little pieces after a long time. But the little pieces will still be in the environment.

☐ Buy products in recyclable containers. As more people buy them, more companies will use them.

☐ Ask the people in charge of your school cafeteria to serve food in reusable dishes and cups.

☐ If you carry your lunch to school, use recyclable containers instead of paper or plastic wrappings. Use a thermos for juice instead of buying waxed boxes, which don't easily degrade.

☐ Ask the people in the school office to use both sides of all paper. Offer to collect usable discarded paper from school wastebaskets and staple it into note pads.

☐ Recycle your own things. Trade books, games and magazines with your friends. Give your outgrown clothes to a younger friend or to a thrift shop. Learn to fix things like a bike tire or a flashlight that you might otherwise throw out.

☐ Join a group like the Children's Rainforest, so you can work with others to preserve the land.

☐ Resolve never to throw out your own hazardous waste—like bug spray cans, oil paint and paintbrush cleaner or mercury batteries—with the rest of the trash. Find out when your town has a collection day for hazardous waste. (If it doesn't have such a collection day, get your family and neighbors to join in and ask for one.)

☐ Plant a tree. Its roots will hold the soil and keep it from washing away. Its leaves or needles will enrich the soil when they fall.

ATMOSPHERE

A layer of air, the atmosphere, surrounds the earth and extends far outward into space. Only the first few miles of atmosphere contain the mixture of gases, mostly oxygen and nitrogen, that all humans, plants and animals need for life. This is the air we breathe from the time we are born until the time we die—the air that all people have breathed since there were people on earth.

Breathing fresh air seems like something no one should have to worry about. But in the last fifty years the atmosphere has become so polluted that many people breathe unhealthy air throughout their entire lives. This polluted atmosphere that surrounds us is changing the whole earth's environment. Oceans and fresh lakes, the land and all living things depend on the earth's atmosphere and are harmed by damage to it. Some of the damage has natural causes, like windstorms and erupting volcanoes. But most is the result of human action.

A thick haze of smog lies over most cities of the world and drifts over the countryside around them for hundreds of miles. The smog comes chiefly from car and truck exhaust and from factories that burn coal. It's also caused by wood-burning stoves, chemical plants, construction materials, dry-cleaning plants and household cleaners. In a lot of places—even in our beautiful national parks—smog spoils the view. But that's not all. Smog can also make you sick. Breathing smoggy air can damage the lungs and cause other health problems, just as smoking cigarettes does. It is especially hard on young children and old people, who are advised to stay indoors in some cities when smog levels are high.

Acid rain is another serious problem: you can't see it in the atmosphere, but you can see what it does around the world. Fish are dying in lakes contaminated by acid rain. Forests are weakened, highways and bridges are corroding and historic buildings—some of them world treasures many centuries old—are crumbling into decay. Acid rain in drinking water affects human health.

Acid rain is made up of invisible particles of sulfur dioxide and nitrogen oxide, gases that are released chiefly from the tall smokestacks of coal-burning electric power plants and from car exhaust. High in the atmosphere these particles interact with moisture and sunlight to become acid-carrying chemicals. They travel over oceans and national borders before falling to earth as acid rain, snow, frost, fog or dew. As countries and states argue about who is to blame for this fallout, the damage worsens.

High above the earth, in the part of the atmosphere called the stratosphere, a layer of natural ozone has been shielding the earth from the sun's ultraviolet radiation for millions of years. Today this ozone layer is thinning. Vast continent-sized "holes," or areas where ozone loss is 50 percent or more, have been discovered over Antarctica in the last decade, and in 1988 an international group of scientists reported a year-round ozone loss of 3 percent over populated areas of the Northern Hemisphere. As more ultraviolet rays reach the earth, they can cause an increase in skin cancer, eye ailments, and other disease in humans, disrupt the growing cycles of crops, damage fish populations in the oceans and affect the earth's weather in ways that are not yet understood.

Smog obscures a city's skyline.

The major cause of ozone depletion is the widespread use of chlorofluorocarbons (CFCs), chemicals made for use in refrigerators and air conditioners, in aerosol sprays and in polystyrene—a plastic foam, used in packaging, that is manufactured by many companies but is best known under the trademark Styrofoam. When CFCs are released they float slowly up to the stratosphere, where the sun's rays break them down, releasing particles of chlorine that destroy ozone. No one is sure how fast ozone is being destroyed and scientists can't predict all the problems that will result. We do know that even if CFC production were stopped today, ozone destruction would continue for a hundred years. That's how long today's CFCs will continue to float up into the stratosphere.

It is not easy to stop production of CFCs. Even though the use of CFCs in aerosol sprays has been banned in the United States and some other countries, these chemicals are still being produced elsewhere. An international treaty to ban production of CFCs will not take full effect until the year 2000. Meanwhile, the ozone layer continues to thin.

Far beneath the ozone layer, a blanket of natural gases in the atmosphere lets the sun's heat through to earth and holds it there, the way glass around a greenhouse holds heat inside. For millions of years, this "greenhouse" blanket has kept the earth warm enough to support life. Today the blanket is thickening and the atmosphere may be warming.

Not all scientists agree on the extent of global warming. But they do agree that human activities have caused an increase of greenhouse

The greenhouse effect.

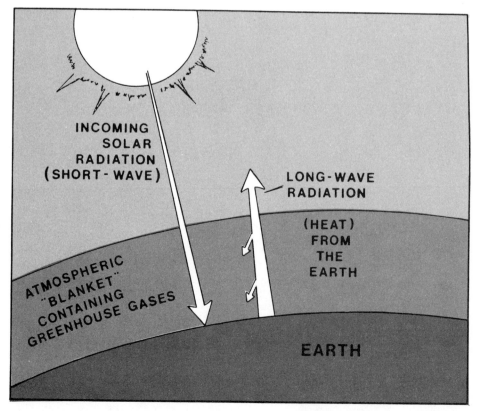

INCOMING SOLAR RADIATION (SHORT-WAVE)

LONG-WAVE RADIATION

(HEAT) FROM THE EARTH

ATMOSPHERIC "BLANKET" CONTAINING GREENHOUSE GASES

EARTH

Cutting down forests adds to the greenhouse effect.

gases in the atmosphere. The burning of fossil fuel—chiefly in cars, incinerators, power plants and factories—releases carbon dioxide, which accounts for approximately one-half of the greenhouse gases. Trees *absorb* carbon dioxide, while the cutting of forests releases still more of it into the atmosphere. Many other gases add to the greenhouse blanket. The same ozone that shields the earth from the sun in the upper atmosphere becomes part of the greenhouse layer closer to earth when it is released by gas-burning engines. The same CFCs that help to break down the ozone layer also contribute to the greenhouse effect. Nitrous oxide, which stays in the atmosphere for centuries, is produced by bacterial action on fertilizers, by forest fires and by the burning of gas and coal. Methane, another gas, is released when bacteria break down organic material in landfills, flooded rice paddies and—believe it or not—the digestive systems of termites and farm animals. The increase in all the greenhouse gases in the atmosphere is the result of the daily activity—particularly the energy use—of the steadily increasing number of people on the earth.

It's hard to predict what the weather will be like tomorrow in any particular place. It's harder still to predict long-term climate change around the world. In spite of several unusually warm years in the 1980s, no one knows for sure whether the earth's temperature is steadily going up, or how much and how fast it might rise in the future. But we do know that even a small rise in the earth's temperature could cause glacial ice to melt, oceans to rise and water to flood the land, bringing vast changes to all life on earth.

Saving the Atmosphere

It isn't easy to clean up the atmosphere. The problems are huge, interconnected and so complex that they are not yet fully understood, even by scientists who have studied them for years.

But the pollution keeps increasing, and today people understand that it is better to be safe than sorry. It is better to work to limit pollution today than to wait until increasing damage to the atmosphere results in problems we cannot now predict.

One big sign of progress is that we now understand that air pollution is a global problem—one that demands international solutions. Today scientists from many countries are working together on problems like the greenhouse effect, and international groups are drawing up laws to protect the atmosphere. Ninety-three nations have agreed to ban production of CFCs by the year 2000, and there is international support for a treaty to limit greenhouse gas production. But this is only a beginning: armed with new reports of greater atmospheric destruction, environmentalists around the world are pressing for far stronger treaties.

People are also working locally—planting trees, cutting down on car use and the use of electric appliances, protesting the spraying of pesticides, refusing to buy products containing CFCs, working to elect candidates who support pollution control—believing that all these actions, together, can help to clear the air.

Planting a tree in the city.

- The Environmental Protection Agency (EPA) estimates that four out of every ten people in the United States live where the air is often unhealthy to breathe.

- On a clear day in Sequoia National Park in California, a visitor can stand on Moro Rock and see for a hundred miles. There are usually only eight or ten clear days a year in the park. On all other days, because of air pollution, visibility is less than ten miles.

- Half of all acid rain deposits in Canada are caused by pollution from U.S. sources.

- More than 2,200 of Sweden's freshwater lakes are almost totally lifeless as a result of acid rain.

- One compact fluorescent light bulb will last ten times longer than a standard light bulb and save a half-ton of the carbon dioxide released by a typical coal-burning power plant as it produces the electricity to light the bulb.

- One mature tree consumes an average of 13 pounds of carbon dioxide per year that would otherwise be freed to pollute the atmosphere. One acre of trees can absorb over two and a half tons of carbon dioxide a year.

- Sales of lightweight pickup trucks and vans (which get only about half the mileage and emit almost twice as much carbon dioxide as cars) are increasing steadily in the United States. Three-quarters of their use is for commuting and shopping—for which a small, fuel-efficient car would do as well.

- The United States has only 5 percent of the world's population, but it is the source of 26 percent of the world's carbon dioxide emissions and 27 percent of the world's CFCs.

- Incinerators that burn garbage release a highly toxic ash that is more of a disposal problem than the garbage itself.

- American companies export 400 to 600 million pounds of pesticides each year. About a quarter of these exports are products that can't be sold in the United States for any use. Many of the rest are sent abroad for uses, like spraying food crops, that are illegal in the United States.

- Billions of pounds of pesticides are used each year in the United States, but a very small amount actually kills pest species, which grow more resistant as more pesticides are used.

■ Kids Against Pollution

What could one fifth-grade class in Closter, New Jersey, do about the earth's polluted atmosphere?

More than the nineteen kids in Mr. Nick Byrne's class at Tenakill School ever expected. They had been studying First Amendment rights—the freedom to speak out. Mr. Byrne had asked them to watch the news on TV and read the newspaper over the weekend and come to class informed about an important issue.

They came to school on Monday not just informed, but also angry about pollution in their state: sludge on New Jersey beaches, solid waste on the land and toxic chemicals in the air.

Somebody said, "Let's *do* something!"

That very morning they formed a group to fight pollution, with themselves as charter members. They named it Kids Against Pollution, or KAP; designed a logo and chose a motto: "Save the Earth, Not Just for Us, But for Future Generations."

Then they set to work. They decided to focus on air pollution and learned all they could about the problem. Then they began to write letters to local newspapers, asking for the enforcement of clean air standards and recycling regulations and for bans on CFCs and incineration. They wrote to schools in every county of their state, sending

The KAP banner at Tenakill School.

*KAP members testify at a govern-
ment hearing.*

material about KAP and asking other classes to join them. They or-
ganized a letter-writing campaign to the governors of New Jersey and
New York—and didn't let the lack of serious replies discourage them.
They kept writing.

The kids of KAP knew that CFCs are released when polystyrene
is made and used and thrown away, so they asked their school board
to ban its use in the school district. The school board agreed to a ban.
So did the town council of Closter—even though polystyrene sup-
pliers fought back. KAP went on to make presentations to county
officials, to the commissioner and staff of the state's EPA and to an
EPA hearing in Washington, D.C.

By now, many people were hearing about KAP. A letter one of
the kids wrote to *Cricket* magazine brought hundreds of replies. KAP
groups were formed around the United States—there are 800 now—
and in foreign countries. (A letter from KAP member Rich Luzzi was
printed in a Russian children's magazine, *Campfire.*) Newspapers and
magazines carried articles about KAP presentations. KAP members
were interviewed on TV and asked to give speeches around the country. Hundreds of people came to their annual Environmental Rights

Days, including the governor, reporters and school groups from as far away as Texas. KAP received awards from business and environmental organizations, from the state of New Jersey, the White House and the United Nations—and each award brought new publicity.

It hasn't all been easy. The KAP founders moved on to sixth grade and then to middle school, and some lost interest. KAP members feel that some adults talk down to them and sometimes media people and politicians act interested just to make themselves look good.

But the Tenakill School provides encouragement. So do KAP parents—who are changing their shopping habits and learning to recycle because of pressure from their kids. These adults are proud of KAP. And the kids are proud of themselves. They're glad for their part in saving the earth—"not just for us, but for future generations."

PROJECTS

Catching Pollution

A One-Week Project

Take some three-by-five-inch index cards and spread a thin layer of Vaseline across one side of each one.

Punch a hole at the end of some of the cards so you can hang them up using a piece of string. Use tape to fasten others.

Find some places where you can leave the cards undisturbed for a week. You might hang them from branches or railings or tape them to windows. Put some near a garage. Tape one to a kitchen or a school-room wall.

At the end of the week, collect the cards. Whatever has stuck to them is a record of the week's visible air pollution in that place.

Car Ad Monitor

A One-Week Project
(With a Ten-Year Follow-up)

Keep a notebook and pencil near the TV set.

Whenever you watch TV, keep a record of each car, station wagon and truck advertisement you see.

For each ad, write down the company name and the name of the model. List the reasons the advertiser gives for buying the vehicle. Beauty? Safety? Speed? Size? Driving pleasure? Low gas mileage?

At the end of the week, count the number of ads that mentioned good mileage. This might tell you how many auto companies are concerned about fuel consumption and its effects on global warming. It might also tell you what consumers want from the cars they buy—or what companies think they want.

Write a letter to each company to praise or to complain about its advertisements.

Save the responses you get. Keep a list of companies that didn't answer.

Write a short report on your project, starting with an explanation of why you are concerned about gas consumption. Send it to your local newspaper.

If the report is printed, you might send copies to the auto companies to which you wrote. Keep a record of those responses, too.

Save all your notes, letters and reports from this project. Write a note to yourself with your prediction of how attitudes to gas consumption will change over the next ten years. Put the material in an envelope with the date on it, marked "Open in Ten Years." Put the envelope in a safe place.

Ten years from now, look back at your records. Then look at the car ads on TV to see how good your predictions were. (By this time, you may have your own driver's license. You may be driving a car that gets 100 miles per gallon. Or you may have decided to ride a bike and take public transportation instead of owning a car at all.)

- [ ] Walk or ride a bike—instead of asking for a ride—to reduce carbon dioxide in the atmosphere.

- [ ] Organize car pools to places you do need a ride to get to, like the mall, a bus stop, a sports event or a party.

- [ ] Don't buy things made of polystyrene, like picnic coolers and plastic cups, which can release chlorofluorocarbons into the atmosphere when they crumble.

- [ ] Don't buy fruits and vegetables, meat or fish packed on polystyrene trays, or eggs in polystyrene cartons. Tell the produce or meat manager and the store manager about the problem with CFCs in packaging. Ask friends to talk to the managers, too.

- [ ] Grow houseplants to absorb carbon dioxide in the air.

- [ ] Make an air freshener with herbs and spices instead of clouding the air with a spray. For really sweet-smelling air, make applesauce or bake bread!

- [ ] Convince your family and your school to switch to fluorescent lights. Find a store that sells the kind of fluorescent bulbs that screw into a standard socket.

- [ ] Plant a tree. If you can, plant two or three. Every tree you plant clears the atmosphere by absorbing carbon dioxide and releasing oxygen. Convince your town to plant more trees. Find articles and photos about other towns with tree-planting projects. Research the costs of planting a tree. Poll store owners and businesspeople to see if they would give money for trees. Write to the newspaper about the project. Get other people involved. Together, you might be able to plant a hundred trees in your town. Five hundred. A thousand!

WATER

THE bright blue color of our planet that we see in photos taken from space comes from the blue of its water. Water covers more than 70 percent of the earth's surface. The continents we live on are really huge islands set in one vast sea that flows around the globe.

Life on earth began in water, billions of years ago, and water sustains all life today. It cycles about endlessly, from rain to streams, from streams to running rivers and from rivers to the seas. Sea water, warmed by the sun's heat, rises to the atmosphere as water vapor, then forms clouds in the cooler air and falls to earth again as rain.

The water in our bodies (each human body is 65 percent water) connects us to this endless cycle. We depend on water and use it in many different ways: we drink it, wash in it, clean with it, cook with it, fish in it and eat fish from it. We use it for irrigation, for transportation and as a source of energy. We splash and swim in it and enjoy just being near it.

We also pollute it.

Onto the natural cycle of water, humans have imposed a cycle of pollution. As the earth's population grows, the results of human activity cloud the water. Acid rain falls from the skies, streams are choked with trash, rivers carry chemicals to the sea, and the water we drink loses its purity.

Water sustains all life.

Polluted water disrupts natural cycles.

The fresh water people use comes from two sources: lakes and rivers on the surface of the land, and water that soaks downward through soil and spongy rock and collects in underground aquifers that can be tapped by wells. We pollute surface water when we pipe wastes directly into it. Surface water and groundwater alike are polluted by this poisonous runoff and by leaks from toxic wastes discarded on the land.

Everything we dump on the land can eventually end up in water: medical waste; salts for deicing roads; toxic chemicals from factories; fertilizers, pesticides and animal waste from agriculture; oil, grease and gasoline; lead and radioactive waste. Some of your own family's waste, like paints and paint thinners, bug sprays, motor oil and household cleaners, may sink into the ground and end up polluting the water you drink.

A bird caught in a plastic six-pack holder.

In most developed countries, organic wastes from sewage are filtered out of drinking water, but hazardous chemicals may still remain. In many developing countries, where people sometimes walk long distances just to get water, what they carry home is likely not to have been treated at all. People may have to drink, wash in and cook with dirty, disease-carrying water.

When sewage and detergents containing phosphates are released into lakes, they encourage the growth of algae, which use up oxygen in the water and choke out other life.

Toxic wastes that run off into streams and rivers often collect in wetlands, where they destroy life and interfere with the wetlands' natural ability to filter and clean the water that flows into them.

Pollution also damages ocean life. For years people have used the ocean as a dump, expecting that everything put into it would flow away, out of sight. Now streams of trash float on the ocean surface, and beaches must be closed when the trash washes up on shore. Much of this refuse is plastic, which can kill sea birds and animals when they get tangled in it or when they mistakenly eat it.

Many kinds of waste end up in lakes, rivers and streams.

Many coastal cities allow raw sewage to flow directly into the ocean. Even when sewage is partially treated before it is dumped, it ends up as a muddy sludge that flows along the ocean floor. It contaminates the microscopic plankton eaten by small fish, the larger fish that eat the small ones, and so on up the food chain to the humans who eat contaminated seafood.

As coastal land is developed and factories are built near the shore, more and more industrial waste is dumped directly into the ocean, joining the toxic wastes already flowing into it from inland waterways. Chemicals from this industrial waste can kill marine life and poison human beings.

Water that's dirty and full of chemicals or waterborne diseases is unsafe to drink. Food that comes from such water is unsafe to eat. Since it takes large amounts of clear water to clean up the dirty water, pollution spoils or uses up much of the earth's water supply.

Oil is a major ingredient of plastics and one of the worst polluters of ocean waters. For years, oil companies have shipped the oil across oceans in tankers so huge that any single accident would be a disaster.

There have been many accidents. The *Exxon Valdez* spill of 1989 destroyed the natural beauty of Prince William Sound in Alaska, killed hundreds of birds and sea animals and polluted nesting grounds for unknown years to come.

People not only pollute the earth's water resources; they also manage them badly. In some places, engineers dam or channel the natural flow of rivers in order to irrigate farm land, but often this diversion takes water away from other places where it is needed just as badly. Rivers, like the atmosphere above them, flow over national boundaries and cannot be controlled by lines on a map. States and individual countries are often at odds with each other over water use and management.

Draining wetlands and covering the land with roads and homes and cities forces rainwater to overflow storm drains and to carry pollutants washed from the streets into streams and rivers. When we destroy wetlands, we also destroy breeding grounds for birds and fish. We lose the wetlands' capacity to purify water; to store heavy flows of storm water that might flood the land; and in dry times, to release stored water into streams and wells.

Damming a river may keep it from flooding downstream, but the dam creates an artificial lake that buries usable land and disrupts the natural flow of streams and the life cycles of many stream animals.

Allowing power plants to take cool water from a river or lake to cool their steam generators and then to release it as warm water changes the oxygen levels in the water's source, killing the fish and plants that live there.

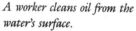

A worker cleans oil from the water's surface.

ABOVE: *Containing the spread of an oil spill.*
BELOW: *Plastic debris clogging a river.*

Swimming is forbidden on a polluted beach.

Allowing people to build power plants—and houses, high-rise apartments, shops and factories—on the shores of rivers and lakes makes it difficult for other people to use the water for recreation, and sometimes even to enjoy the view.

There is not an endless supply of water. Rain does not fall continually. To support constantly growing populations, we need more fresh water than we get from the skies. But every time a factory uses water to produce goods, every time one person flushes a toilet, the supply of fresh water in a stream or a reservoir is lowered and our precious supply of fresh groundwater is reduced.

In many parts of the earth, people are using up groundwater faster than it can be replenished. In some places, water is so scarce that only a very few crops can grow. It is difficult for people who live in those places to survive. They are desperate for water. Just having enough fresh water to drink would seem like a blessing. Wasting it thoughtlessly would almost seem a crime.

Saving Water

There are ways that we can preserve the usable amounts of water we have. We can make laws to protect it, like the Clean Water Act in the United States or the regulations passed by the United Nations to protect the earth's oceans. But laws must be enforced to be effective. Right now, industries around the world are breaking water pollution laws. It is crucial for citizens to learn about the laws and to pressure companies to comply with them and politicians to enforce them.

Industries are not the only polluters and wasters of water. An enormous amount of waste goes on in people's homes. We need to understand that each gallon of water we waste lowers the water level in a lake or reservoir, and that each gallon we pollute seeps down into groundwater or flows off into a river or an ocean.

Just about everyone knows that a single toilet flush uses five to seven gallons of water, that watering a lawn in the middle of the day is wasteful, that it's stupid to let water run while you're brushing your teeth or washing the dishes. We know how to save water. The important thing is deciding to do it—today and every day.

Water is a renewable resource, but it can take hundreds of years for a lake or aquifer to clean and purify itself. Every drop of water we save preserves the supply of clear water that supports us now and that will support future generations.

The pleasure of fresh water.

- Approximately 97 percent of the earth's water is in the oceans, and 2 percent is ice. All the fresh water that people use comes from the last 1 percent.

- Almost 80 percent of all living matter is in the oceans.

- Nearly 100 million tons of plastic end up in the ocean every year. A plastic six-pack holder has a life expectancy of 450 years.

- More than 90 percent of the world's drinkable water comes from a source under the surface of the earth (ground-water).

- In the United States, nearly 500,000 acres of surface wetlands, most of it freshwater wetlands, are lost each year.

- U.S. industries produce more than 60,000 synthetic chemicals. Many of them are toxic and all of them can be carried in or on flowing water.

- Because of industrial toxic waste, almost all the water in Poland's rivers is unfit to drink.

- A person can live for weeks without food, but cannot live for more than a few days without water.

- A faucet dripping at the rate of one drop per second wastes 880 gallons of water a year.

- Every ton of recycled paper saves 7,000 gallons of water that would be used in paper production.

- About one-quarter of all wastewater is dumped into the ocean.

- The oceans supply 60 billion tons of food each year.

- Israel uses 35 percent of the wastewater from its cities, after treatment, to irrigate its fields.

■ Saving the Coast

There are 260 miles of coastline in the state of Delaware. Every year, kids from schools around the state come to Lewes Beach to save one small part of this coastline and to learn how to preserve all of it.

They come to the Children's Beach House, a place where kids study the ocean by wading into it. Kids who can't wade in ride wheelchairs to the water's edge, pulling crab traps along to collect live sea creatures, like crabs, snails, starfish and minnows.

Everyone learns about the coastal environment of Delaware—a state where no place is more than eight miles away from tidal water. They learn about the tidal marshes that nourish ocean life and about the sand dunes that protect beaches from storm tides and high waves. They hear about the birds and sea animals that die when they get caught in six-pack rings or swallow plastic bags, and they see for themselves how litter and pollution can spoil the beach's beauty.

Then they set to work.

Every group that comes to the Beach House helps to clean up a stretch of public beach nearby. They collect the trash that people have dropped carelessly, stuffing what they find into bags and pails.

Some groups work on the sand dunes. They've learned that even large dunes will shift and disappear as the wind blows sand off them unless there is something to hold the sand in place.

Beach grass will hold it. Grass slows the force of the wind and traps the windblown sand grains, making the dunes grow higher. Underground, a network of beach-grass rhizomes, or stems, helps to hold the dune in place.

A Children's Beach House work team.

Beach-grass rhizomes spread naturally by themselves, but they don't spread fast enough to keep up with wind erosion. To stop this erosion, you have to plant a lot of beach grass. On Lewes Beach you can't plant it by machines—that only works in large, flat places. Most dune erosion in Delaware is in small, sloping areas. So kids plant the grass themselves. They do it in teams of four: a plant bucket carrier, a spader, a plant feeder and a planter.

First, they mark a straight row with string. Then the spader digs a hole twelve to fourteen inches deep, holding the spade in it to keep the sand out. The plant feeder measures out fertilizer and spreads it in a circle around the hole. The plant bucket carrier gives three grass plants to the planter, who sets them in the hole. The spader pulls out the spade. The planter packs the sand around the plants until it's so firm that they won't come out.

That's how you do one plant. After they've planted a whole row, the team moves the marker and starts on a new one. They keep going like this, changing jobs every thirty plants, until they have planted 120.

It's hard work. But it's good.

"We helped to save the beach," one planter said afterward.

"We put our names in the sand," said the spader.

"We had a good time," said the plant bucket carrier.

"I hope we can go back to plant more grass," said the plant feeder.

They are going back. They're going to see how the grass they planted has spread over the sand of their Delaware beach. They're going to plant more grass, to save more dunes for the future.

Planting beach grass.

Cleaning up Adobe Creek.

■ Fish Story

Ninety years ago, the last steelhead spawned in Adobe Creek in Petaluma, California. The steelhead is a silvery rainbow trout that migrates to the Pacific before returning to fresh water to spawn. Ninety years ago the city diverted the stream's water for its use, leaving the creek only spillage from winter rains. Adobe Creek was dry and dead, a dump for the trash people tossed into it—tires, mattresses, appliances, garbage.

Five years ago, a group of Casa Grande High School students called the United Anglers were determined to bring the steelhead back to Adobe Creek. Working on weekends, they cleared away the tons of garbage, piece by piece. They planted hundreds of young trees to stop shore erosion. They dug out the gravel creekbed to create safe spawning grounds. Finally, they turned an unused greenhouse behind the school into a fish hatchery. Several thousand fingerlings hatched from the first batch of eggs, and on a day when winter runoff filled the creek, the Anglers notched the fish's fins for identification and let them go.

On a rainy spring day, three students walking on the bank saw a flitting shadow in the ripples. A fish! As the United Anglers gathered at the creek, they saw a notch in the fish's fin—proof that it was one they had released. They had brought the steelhead back.

Now the Anglers have begun a new project—building a new fish hatchery. With car washes and other projects, they have raised half the money it will cost, and construction has begun. Meanwhile, more than half of the original group have gone on to college to prepare for environmental careers. All of them are committed to preserving the environment.

They know how to do it. They know they *can* do it.

PROJECTS

Stop the Drip

An Overnight Project

If there is a leaky faucet in your home, put a container under it to catch the drip. Leave it overnight. You may be surprised to see how much water collects overnight from even a slow drip.

It is definitely worth fixing every leaky faucet. You'll save water and you'll save money.

If you don't know how to fix a faucet, you can learn how from a book. Find one in the library.

Check the Flow

A One-Minute Project

How much water runs out of your sink faucet in a minute?

All you have to do to find out is put a pail in the sink. Turn the water on and let it run while you time it. . . .

Stop!

What you see in the pail is the water that would have run down the sink in just one minute, while you were rinsing off a dish or washing a potato.

This time you saved it. (Use the water you have just saved to water the houseplants.) Next time, you can save water by rinsing or scrubbing in a small pan of water.

Catch a Shower

A Five-Minute Project

Which uses more water, a bath or a shower?

To find out, plug the drain of the tub and take a five-minute shower.

Then check the water level in the tub. Is it as deep as the water you usually run for a bath?

If you can convince your family to get a water-saver shower head, you should try the experiment after you've installed it to see how much lower the water level is.

Cool It

A Two-Minute Project

How much water is used for drinking when you let the water run till it's cool?

To find out, put a clean pot in the sink and turn the water on. Let it run till it's cool. Then turn the faucet off.

The amount of water in the pot is the amount you waste with each cool drink.

You'll save that same amount with each drink if you keep a bottle of cold tap water in the refrigerator for drinking.

(Use the water you caught in the pot to wash dishes, vegetables or your hands.)

- [ ] Learn how to fix leaks—and fix them. You'll save a lot of water.

- [ ] Find a plastic bottle that will fit in your toilet tank without blocking moving parts. Fill it with water and a few stones. Less water will now be used when you flush.

- [ ] Don't keep the water running while you wash your hands or brush your teeth. Turn the faucets on and off instead.

- [ ] Take shorter showers.

- [ ] If your family uses a washing machine or dishwasher, take charge of making sure they're only run with full loads. (You can wash a few dishes by hand if you need them.)

- [ ] Find out about safe products for laundry and household cleaning. Ask adults you live with to try them.

- [ ] If your family has a car, make sure not to dump out old oil when the oil is changed. Take it to a gas station for recycling.

- [ ] Don't use chemical fertilizers or pesticides, which pollute streams as they run off in rainwater. Learn about organic substitutes.

- [ ] Don't dump leftover toxic products down a sewer or into a trash can. Find out where in your town you can get rid of them safely. If your town doesn't have such a place, ask why.

- [ ] If you have a back yard, put out containers to catch rainwater. Use it to water flowers.

- [ ] Plant flowers, trees and shrubs that are native to the climate where you live. They will do well with less water than non-native plants.

- [ ] Water gardens in the late afternoon or the early morning, so water doesn't evaporate in the heat of the sun.

- [ ] Plant a tree. Trees store water and release it slowly into the ground, keeping it from running off with valuable nutrients.

ENERGY

ENERGY is the force that makes things work. It's the force of the wind turning the blades of a windmill. It's the force of the sun warming what it touches; it's the force of your legs walking on the ground or pedaling a bike. It's the force of giant power plants that create electricity and the force of gas that runs a car engine.

We can't see energy. But its effects surround us from morning to night. It takes energy to keep a house warm, a refrigerator running, lights burning and the TV on. It takes energy to move cars and trucks along the highways and planes across the sky. It takes energy to run the factories that make what we buy to wear and read and play with and eat. It takes energy to collect, sort, burn, cart off, crush, bury and find new places to bury all the things we buy, unwrap, use and throw away.

The chief sources of energy in the world are fossil fuels—coal, oil and natural gas—and wood. (Most electricity, another major source of energy, is created by coal-burning plants.) When fossil fuels are burned, they release huge amounts of greenhouse gases as well as toxic fallout and acid rain into the atmosphere. The more energy we use, even in such everyday acts as driving a car, taking a hot shower or turning on a light, the more pollution we help to cause. (One-third of all energy use—and therefore one-third of energy pollution—in the United States comes from homes and cars.)

The industrialized nations of the world consume vast quantities of oil. Conflict over control of oil resources is a major problem in the world today. Wars are fought over access to oil, while nations fail to adopt policies that conserve it. Pollution is an inevitable result of overdependence on fossil fuels.

Pollution isn't the only cost of retrieving energy from oil and coal. Other costs are the destruction of land and forests by coal mining and the lasting damage from giant oil spills, like the *Exxon Valdez* disaster in 1989, which destroyed the natural ecology of the region.

Using fossil fuels means using them up. They are nonrenewable; nature can't re-create them at anywhere near the rate at which people are using them up today. Sometime in the future, all of them will run out. We will need other, renewable, energy sources.

*Huge cities use
vast amounts of energy.*

Grand Coulee Dam.

Some are available now. One is water, which has been used to create energy for thousands of years. Today hydropower, generated by huge dams, is a major source of electricity in many parts of the world. But hydropower has its own costs. When dams are built, the area above them is flooded, sometimes for miles. In some places people lose their homes as well as the rich river soil in which they once grew crops. In other places, wonderful wild landscapes are buried forever under new, artificial lakes. Below the dams, the natural habitat of fish and wildlife in the river valley is destroyed as the course of the river is changed.

Solar energy—the use of the sun's power—is another renewable source of energy. In the 1970s, many nations of the world supported the development of solar energy, which is clean and easy to install. In the United States, solar collectors were added to old homes and built into new ones to take advantage of the sun's heat. Homeowners found their heating costs were sharply reduced. But in the 1980s, when oil prices dropped, the United States cut tax support for solar installations and solar research, and a good opportunity to develop this renewable substitute for fossil fuel was lost. The United States continues to be oil-dependent in the 1990s, and access to oil is a major source of international conflict.

Another alternative source of energy available today is nuclear power, created when uranium atoms are split into fragments that create energy waves called radiation. Forty years ago, nuclear power was seen as the hope of the future. Nuclear power was "clean"—it didn't pol-

Nuclear waste.

lute the atmosphere, add to the greenhouse effect or cause acid rain. Some people thought it would be so cheap to produce electricity from nuclear plants that there would be no need for electric meters—everyone could have it free.

Nuclear power turned out to have serious problems even beyond what turned out to be the huge costs of building and running nuclear plants. A nuclear plant is only "clean" if nothing goes wrong with it. But something *has* gone wrong: there is a growing number of nuclear accidents around the world in which poisonous radioactive materials have been released into the atmosphere and fallen to earth to contaminate soil and water. A major accident in 1986 at the Chernobyl nuclear plant in the Soviet Union caused the death and serious illness of workers and people nearby, the evacuation of neighboring towns and the contamination of crops and farm animals in the Soviet Union and Europe. It will be years before the effects of this accident are fully known.

Even when a nuclear plant runs without accident, its used fuel produces radioactive waste that no one yet knows how to get rid of safely. Some of this radioactive waste will continue to be dangerous for centuries. Much of it now sits in storage tanks of cooled water while scientists debate how to dispose of it so it can never again come into contact with people. Even burying it deep within a mountain (one of the likeliest plans) has risks: What if an earthquake shakes the mountain? What if underground water seeps into it? There is too much nuclear waste in the world right now, without making more.

Saving Energy

It's clear that developed countries cannot keep on making and using energy as they do now without endangering the health of the planet. But it's understandable that people in developing countries want some of the benefits that energy brings to developed ones.

RIGHT: *For centuries, wind power has provided energy for farming.*
BELOW: *A building designed to benefit from winter sun and summer shade.*

There are three main ways to meet the world's present and future energy needs: cleaning up the ways energy is produced; improving or inventing other, less damaging ways to make it; and saving it.

Cleaning up existing energy plants is costly and only partly effective. It is possible to filter out some of the pollution from coal-burning smokestacks, but there is no known way to reduce the emission of carbon dioxide, just as there is no known way to clean up nuclear waste.

It's clear that we can learn to create energy in less damaging ways than with fossil fuels or nuclear power. Some alternative ways are now known. Solar power is one important source of energy. The sun's power can also be used to generate electricity through chemical reactions in photovoltaic cells. Wind power is another source of energy, and so is heat from within the earth—geothermal energy. Other sources of energy like biomass—plant and animal wastes—have been used for centuries around the world. Today we need to find inexpensive and easy ways to develop these energy sources for widespread use.

There is only one sure way to solve the world's energy problem, and that is by using less of it. Those who use the most energy now are most responsible for cutting back. We can do it. We have to learn how to use energy more efficiently to heat and cool buildings and run machines and appliances and cars. We have to get used to thinking about the energy we're using as we use it in our everyday lives, and to keep the idea of saving it always in our minds. We don't need to invent energy-saving machines—we can *be* them!

A house with solar heating panels on its roof.

- In one year, people on the earth use up the amount of fossil fuel it took one million years to produce.

- The United States has 5 percent of the world's population, but uses 26 percent of the world's oil.

- According to the U.S. Department of Energy, an average American household consumes energy equal to 1,253 gallons of oil per year.

- If every household in the United States lowered its average heating temperature six degrees for 24 hours, we could save more than 570,000 barrels of oil.

- Every ton of recycled paper saves 4,100 kilowatt-hours of electricity—enough energy to heat the average home for six months.

- The paper industry is the single largest user of fuel oil in the United States. It's the third-largest energy consumer.

- The amount of used motor oil dumped in the United States each year is more than the amount of oil that leaked from the *Exxon Valdez*.

- More energy leaks through American windows every year than flows through the Alaskan pipeline as oil.

- In some parts of Africa women and children spend 300 days out of the year collecting wood for cooking.

- The Netherlands has over 9,000 miles of bike paths.

- In China there are 540 bicycles for every car.

■ Dumplings

Years ago, kids used to hunt for treasure at the town dump. They never knew what they would find—a bicycle seat or a workable clock, or maybe a top hat to wear on Halloween.

Kids still never know what they'll find in a dump—but today it's likely to be hazardous, poisonous and dangerous to their health. Few people would want to take anything home from one. Most people would be horrified to have a town dump near a school.

Not in Shrewsbury, Vermont. The Shrewsbury dump (or transfer station) is different. It's a place where trash is sorted, compacted and recycled. It's not disgusting or dangerous, and it's just a short walk from the Shrewsbury Mountain School.

Kids at the Mountain School learn to recycle from kindergarten on. Every class has bins for white and colored wastepaper, and there's a compost cart in the hall for lunch trash. All the compost goes into a compost pile at the dump. The whole school has a special attitude about saving and reusing things. They always try to recycle or reuse things instead of throwing them out.

"Nobody just tosses stuff out around here," says sixth-grader Jason Grace. "Kids go more to the recycling box than to the garbage."

George Brigham, manager of the Shrewsbury dump, built the school's recycling boxes, made the compost cart from recycled parts and thinks it's great that the school kids are enthusiastic about recycling. He calls them "dumplings." Every summer there's a Dumpling Jamboree at the dump, with games and contests and, naturally, lots of dumplings to eat.

It's fun. But for the kids of Mountain School, recycling is more than just fun. A third-grader explained why: "It makes me feel like I'm doing something for the earth."

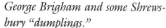

George Brigham and some Shrewsbury "dumplings."

Back and Forth to the Future

*A One-Hour Project
(With a One-Hour, and a Fifty-
Year, Follow-up)*

Make a list of all the electric appliances in your home.

Start in the kitchen and try to list each one: Electric stove? Refrigerator? Dishwasher? Microwave oven? Can opener? Blender? Coffee grinder? Coffee maker? Toaster? Juicer? Electric clock? Your kitchen may hold one or two of these, all of these, or more.

Next, list the electric appliances in other rooms of your home. Go slowly to be sure you catch everything. Do you have an electric toothbrush? A computer? A lamp? An iron? A vacuum cleaner?

After you've made your list, go through it and put an *X* beside the things you wouldn't like to live without.

Go through the list again. This time put an asterisk (*) beside the things you really couldn't get along without.

Maybe you'll decide not to use up energy on the ones that aren't as important to you.

For the follow-up, you need to talk with some people who are 70 years old or more—relatives, or neighbors or friends.

Show them your list.

Ask how many of the appliances on it they had when they were your age.

Ask how they got along without the ones they didn't have. You might get some good energy-saving ideas. You might also hear some interesting stories about life without electricity.

Can you predict how people will be using electricity when you're 70 years old?

- Will they have more appliances, or fewer?
- Will electricity be cheaper, or more expensive?
- What kinds of energy will run appliances and tools?
- Will people still care about saving energy?

Write your predictions on a piece of paper, put it into a tightly sealed jar and bury it in a place you're likely to come back to when you're around 70 years old.

Maybe you'll find a future kid to tell your stories to.

Do It Yourself

An Ongoing Project

Use *your* energy to save energy! Here's how:

Start a collection of tools, gadgets, toys and appliances that don't use electricity or battery power. You probably have some in your house now—a hand-turned pencil

sharpener or a can opener. You may have others, like a little-kid's pull toy, an outdoor clothesline, an old lawn mower, or, if you're lucky, an old-time hand-cranked ice cream maker. See how many more you can collect from relatives, thrift shops, or even from the trash other people throw out on collection days.

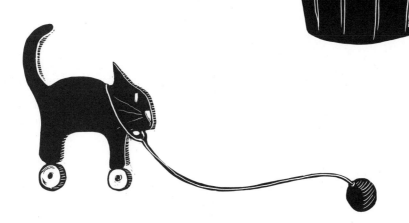

You could write an article for your school or town newspaper about saving energy this way.

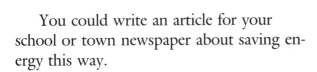

Stacks of Racks

A Yearlong Project

You know that it saves energy and pollution to ride a bike to the store or the library instead of going there in a car. It also makes you more independent if you don't have to ask someone for a ride.

But what do you do with your bike when you get where you're going?

You could start a bike-rack campaign in your town. Get other people to work with you—kids in your class or scout group or club.

Begin with some research:

Where would bike racks be helpful?
How many people would use them? (Ask adults as well as kids.)
How much do bike racks cost? Is it cheaper if you buy a number of them at one time?
Who would pay for the bike racks?
Who would install them?
Would your town support a bike-rack project?

How much time would you and your friends contribute to the project?

Let people know what you've found out:

Talk to community groups: the Chamber of Commerce, the library association, the police department, the PTA.
Write letters to the newspaper.
Contact the radio or television station.
Speak at a meeting of your town's planning board.

As you work on the project, keep a record of your progress. Take photographs of your interviews and presentations, and any money-raising activities. Take more photos when the bike racks are installed (and be sure to take pictures of people riding). At the end, write up the project. You might convince people in another town to start one like yours.

The Big Wrap-up

A Ten-Minute Project

Try this when you return home from grocery shopping.

Put an empty paper bag on the table or counter where you're unpacking the groceries.

As you put things away, throw any extra wrappings—plastic bags, freezer bags, paper bags, cartons—into the empty bag.

How full is the bag? Empty it on a table to see what you've got.

It took energy to make each one of those wrappings. When you throw them out, it will take more energy to get rid of them.

How many pieces of wrapping in the pile could you save to use again?

CHECKLIST

☐ Recycle! Convince your family, your school and your town to separate papers, metal, plastics and other garbage, and to recycle, compost and reuse as much trash as possible.

☐ Make a list of all disposable items that you and your family use every day. Resolve to stop using some of them.

☐ Take charge of turning off lights in your house when they aren't needed.

☐ Ask people in your family to consider solar-powered appliances if they're buying a calculator, battery recharger or outdoor light.

☐ If you have a dishwasher or washing machine, only run them with full loads. Offer to load them yourself to be sure.

☐ If you have a clothes dryer, use it only when the weather is bad. Offer to hang clothes outside at other times yourself. Make sure your dryer has a dryer exhaust to keep warm, moist, dryer air indoors.

☐ If you live in a house, take charge of turning down the thermostat at night or when people aren't home. Experiment with wearing more clothes (long underwear is good) and keeping the thermostat five or six degrees lower.

☐ If you're in a place (movie theater, dentist's office, school) that feels uncomfortably hot—or too cold from air conditioning—speak up. Ask people near you if the temperature bothers them. Ask someone in charge to adjust it.

☐ If there are farm stands or green markets near you, ask your family to buy food there. You'll help to save the energy it takes to truck food a long distance—and the things you buy will be fresher and tastier. Maybe you could ride your bike there.

☐ Find out how to get a free energy audit. Urge your family or landlord and your school principal to request one.

☐ Whether you live in a house or an apartment, offer to put weatherstripping putty in the cracks around your windows.

🌳 Urge your family or your landlord to plant trees near the south and west windows of your house or apartment building to keep it cool in the summer. Offer to help with the planting.

PLANTS & ANIMALS

No one knows the number of plant and animal species on earth. Scientists have given names to about one and a half million varieties of life, and they estimate that the total number, including the unnamed species, is close to four million. Every one of these millions of species of plants and animals—and each distinct organism within it—is a part of the web of life that has existed since life itself began on earth. Each carries life onward into the future, for as long as life exists.

All this great variety of life, from the smallest mite to the largest tree, is sustained by one basic source: the energy of the sun. Each organism uses this energy, or food produced with this energy, to transform nonliving matter into new living tissues and structures. The organism develops as part of the environment around it, following patterns in its genes passed on over millions of years of trial and error, change and pause. By existing, reproducing and, in the end, by dying and decaying, each distinct and special plant and animal contributes to the endless recycling of life on earth and to the amazing diversity of the earth's species.

It has taken hundreds of millions of years for this diversity of species to develop. Over that expanse of time, some species became extinct—they disappeared from the earth—and many new species developed. Slow increases in species diversity were set back by environmental changes that caused the mass extinction of species; there appears to have been a huge climate change that caused the extinction of dinosaurs sixty million years ago. But after each setback, the number of species increased dramatically. By the time the human species came into being, there was a greater variety of species on the earth than ever before in its history.

Today, that amazing diversity of species is disappearing. Our one human species is multiplying so fast and altering the earth's environment so severely that we have caused the extinction of thousands of other species that once shared life on earth with us.

For 600 million years the rate of extinction was only about one species each year. But at this moment in earth's history—right now, while you are reading this book—one species a *day* is vanishing, and the rate is accelerating steadily toward one species an *hour*. Many biologists fear that by the year 2000 more than one-fifth of all the species of life on earth could vanish.

This beetle and the monkey on the facing page illustrate part of the nearly half of the earth's species that live in tropical rain forests.

These extinctions are happening all over the earth. Rare species of plants and animals are disappearing before we can even discover and describe them. Each endangered species of bear or owl or flower or grain that we hear about is just one of a vast, unknown total of species nearing extinction. And as we damage and pollute our environment we endanger countless more.

Every species on earth lives in a specific environment, or ecosystem, with its own climate, altitude and soil and water characteristics. The ecosystem—a community of plants and animals that are dependent on each other—can be as small as a decaying log or as large as a vast rain forest. This environment steadily regenerates itself as its plants transform the sun's energy into food by the process called photosynthesis. The relationships of species to each other within their ecosystems are astonishingly complex, even in examples as familiar to us as robins and earthworms, squirrels and nuts, or humans and the living source of hamburgers.

When people damage or pollute an ecosystem, they interfere with these relationships in ways that can destroy whole species. Sometimes the destruction is direct: human hunters killed the seemingly endless numbers of buffalo that once roamed the North American plains, until all but a few had vanished. Hunters brought the passenger pigeon to extinction. Rhinoceros and elephants and many species of birds and fish are still directly endangered by hunting.

Human activity endangers other species in ways that may seem less direct but are just as damaging. Land development destroys and paves over some species' natural habitats. Pollution and dredging threatens ocean species. Pesticides kill far more varieties of insects than those they are meant to reach, and pesticide runoff endangers many kinds of animals and fish. Acid rain and smog endanger countless species. The human development of nuclear weapons, with the danger of accidents, waste disposal and especially potential use, still threatens all species on earth.

The greatest rate of species extinction since the dinosaurs disappeared is taking place today in the tropical rain forests that circle the equator. These wet, lush forests, with their tall tree canopies and thick undergrowth, cover only 7 percent of the earth's surface, but they are home to nearly half of all its species. Now they are being cut and burned—at the rate of a hundred acres a minute—to provide logs for export to many countries around the world and in some cases living and farming space for expanding populations. In Central America, forests are cleared to make pastures for the raising of cattle, with much of the beef ending up as hamburgers served in fast-food restaurants in the United States.

Clearing the rain forests destroys these ancient ecosystems and the millions of rare, beautiful and useful species of plants and animals that

Destroyed rain forest.

live within them. The destruction of trees produces great quantities of carbon dioxide from the material of the forests and releases it into the atmosphere to add to the earth's warming. It allows huge amounts of the world's fresh water to run off, carrying the forest topsoil away. Clearing the forest allows poor farm workers to move in and plant crops on the land—but only for a year or two, until sparse nutrients in the soil are used up. Without forest cover to shade and replenish the soil, the complex ecosystem of the rain forest is destroyed.

We have just begun to understand what the loss of any ecosystem, like a tropical rain forest, means for our own species, for our many human cultures and for the earth. With its destruction there is the loss of people's livelihood and culture. There is the loss of scientific adventure and discovery. There is the loss of biological history—each vanished plant or creature within the system represents a unique pattern of genes that once existed and now is gone forever. There is the loss of our human joy in diversity itself—the dazzling combinations of color, pattern, shape and function within the variety of earth's living species. And there is the loss of future diversity, for without each vanished species, its unique combination of genes is no longer available to adapt to unknown future circumstances and needs.

To some people it seems outrageous to halt a construction project or an industry that could provide thousands of jobs because the work endangers a single species. But often, the near-extinction of one species serves as a warning that an entire ecosystem, with all the jobs it provides, is endangered. So a headline like "Spotted Owl vs. 20,000 Jobs" is unhelpful. The economic health of the Pacific Northwest is not separate from the health of old-growth forests and the hundreds of species, including the spotted owl, that live in them. Protecting people's jobs depends on preserving the environment.

Each endangered species is a part of the complex web of life that has adapted to earth's environment over millions of years. Together, these species make up a storehouse of genetic information. Scientists use this information every day. They combine genes of existing plants to develop crops that can grow in poor soil and low rainfall to feed earth's growing population. They create medicines—70 percent of the plants useful in cancer treatment are found only in the rain forests—that can reduce disease and lessen pain. With the loss of any species we risk the loss of a yet-unknown benefit to human beings.

But there is an even more basic reason to preserve species diversity: With every species loss, we humans lose part of that sense of connection to the earth that *makes* us human. To value each species is to respect the life that flows through us—life we share with all the life on earth. Australian aboriginal Bill Neidjie of the Bunitz clan expresses the idea this way:

> *Tree . . .*
> *he watching you.*
> *You look at tree,*
> *he listen to you.*
> *He got no finger,*
> *he can't speak.*
> *But that leaf . . .*
> *he pumping, growing,*
> *growing in the night.*
> *While you sleeping*
> *you dream something.*
> *Tree and grass same thing.*
> *They grow with your body,*
> *with your feeling.*

Saving Plants and Animals

We are beginning to understand what the loss of species diversity can mean to the earth, and we are trying to slow its pace.

Scientists are making heroic attempts to count and name and describe new species and to save their ecosystems so others can appreciate their diversity.

Citizens are taking action against pollution—not only for the sake of other humans, but for the sake of all species.

Many of us are changing our diets as we learn that what we eat makes a difference. Statistics show us that the resources needed to raise animals for meat are far greater than what is needed to grow grain. Eating low on the food chain—eating more grains and vegetables directly instead of using them as animal feed—seems sensible and right when we know that sixty million hungry people could live adequately on the grain and soybeans that would be saved if everyone in the United States ate 10 percent less meat. Not everyone will become a vegetarian, but most people have begun to eat less meat.

Many people today are joining organizations that work to save the earth's rain forests. We have begun to understand that when rain forests disappear, the earth's climate changes, and soil depletion, species loss and poverty result. The destruction goes on, but we can hope that world-wide awareness will preserve some rain forests for the future.

Meanwhile, people who live in rain forests continue to use them in the old ways that preserve the forest ecosystem: growing crops in small areas; harvesting fruit, nuts and oil; and tapping rubber from trees. Scientists and governments around the world are beginning to learn from these native people, instead of blindly destroying their traditional way of life.

Finally, governments are taking first steps to reduce their stockpiles of nuclear weapons, partly because of pressure from ordinary citizens. And citizens in every country will keep up the pressure until the threat of nuclear war, with its inevitable species extinction, no longer exists.

A demonstration against nuclear weapons.

- Since 1900, over 86 percent of all known varieties of apple have become extinct.

- Less than 10 percent of the ancient forests that once stretched from California to Alaska remain today.

- Ninety acres of Alaska's rain forest are cut down each day.

- The burning of slash left after clear-cutting forests is the largest source of air pollution in the Pacific Northwest.

- Rain forests cover only 7 percent of the land on earth, but they contain nearly half of all the trees on earth.

- More than half of the total number of species on earth live in tropical rain forests.

- Almost half the birds that breed in North America each year fly south to winter in tropical forests in Mexico, South America, Central America and the Caribbean.

- The rain forest is being cut down at the rate of one football field every second. Every hour of the day, 500,000 rain forest trees are cut down.

- In 1970 there were 52 endangered species in the United States; in 1989 there were 539.

- Of all the animal species on earth, 40 percent are beetles.

- One-third of all the grain harvested on earth today is fed to livestock and poultry.

- It takes sixteen pounds of grain and soy to turn out just one pound of beef. It takes six pounds of grain and soy to get a pound of pork, four pounds for a pound of turkey and three pounds for a pound of eggs or a pound of chicken.

- Every year, drift net fleets leave about 500–600 miles of net floating in the North Pacific. Every year, an estimated 800,000 seabirds become entangled in the nets and die.

- Approximately 50,000 northern fur seals are drowned each year by lost plastic fishing net.

- In 15 species of seabirds found on Midway Island in the Pacific, 100 percent of the chicks had bits of latex balloons in the gut.

- Scientists say that one in three species or subspecies of native freshwater fish in North America is now or may soon be threatened by the degradation of lakes, rivers and streams.

- An estimated 100,000 grizzly bears once roamed the lower 48 states of the United States. Fewer than 1,000 are left today.

A rain forest in Costa Rica.

■ The Children's Rainforest

Half of all plant and animal species on earth live in the tropical rain forests. Bright birds, rare mammals, sweet-smelling ferns and flowers and myriads of strange insects exist together in the lush green layers beneath the canopies of giant trees. Like other forests, rain forests clear the earth's atmosphere as they soak up carbon dioxide and convert it to oxygen.

But today these ancient rain forests are being cut down and burned at a rate so fast that scientists predict all of them will vanish within a century. Once it has been destroyed, a rain forest is gone forever. It will never come back.

When kids hear this, they want to do something about it. Children in different parts of the world *are* doing something. They're buying their own small pieces of rain forest land, to save it from destruction. They're putting the pieces together to create the Children's Rainforest.

Many of them first heard about the rain forest from a biologist named Sharon Kinsman, who studies plants and their flowers and pollinators in Costa Rica for part of the year and teaches at Bates College in Maine for the rest of it.

Sharon Kinsman believes that the destruction of rain forest is one of earth's major problems. A few years ago she went to Sweden to work on rain forest research and conservation with other concerned scientists. One day she visited a little country school and showed the students slides of the frogs and monkeys and flowers of a tropical rain forest. She explained that all the earth's rain forest was disappearing—fast.

"We should save some forest!" the children said.

"I know one to save," Dr. Kinsman said. She told them how much an acre in Costa Rica's Monteverde rain forest would cost. In a few days, the children wrote a play about the rain forest and earned enough money from admissions to save fourteen acres.

Before long, students all over Sweden were joining in. The Children's Rainforest had begun.

Now thousands of children in at least twenty states in the United States and from at least ten other countries have joined together to save the rain forest. They are walking, talking, making plays and posters, selling books and tree seedlings, collecting pennies and earning money from work to add acres to the Children's Rainforest, a lush undisturbed forest near the Monteverde Cloud Forest Reserve.

Spreading the word about the Children's Rainforest.

In Huntington Beach, California, sixth-grader Ryan Miller of Schroeder School described his class's project:

One thing that meant a lot to me is the rain forest that my class created. It was really cool. Everybody reported on an endangered rain forest animal. Then we made trees, vines and all our animals out of paper. We invited all the other classes in our school to tour our rain forest. With the plastic bottles and cans we saved, our class raised money to buy one acre of tropical rain forest in the Monteverde area of Costa Rica. We are proud of our contribution to saving the Earth.

In Farmington, Maine, ten-year-old Matty Goodman wrote a leaflet, organized his friends, made a rain forest banner and a parrot costume and became an official entry in the annual Fourth of July parade. "Nearly 40 million acres have been destroyed since last July fourth," Matty's leaflet said. ". . . Even though it is very far away, the rain forest is important to all of us."

Rain forests are vanishing fast. But some will be preserved, because children are helping to save them.

■ Wolf Quest

"When I think of wolves, I think of stories like 'Little Red Riding Hood' and movies like *Teen Wolf.* . . ."

"When I think of wolves, I think of bats, snakes and spiders. They are all mean!"

Most of the kids in the fifth grade of Mead School in Wisconsin Rapids, Wisconsin, felt that way about wolves—until they began to study them.

They learned how wolves raise their young, how they communicate and how they hunt for food. They found that wolves help to maintain the population and strengthen the herds of deer, elk and moose by preying on weak, old and sick animals. They came to see the timber wolf as a beautiful wild species and a valuable part of the Wisconsin ecosystem. They learned that there were once thousands of wolves in the state, but that people had killed so many that by 1960 wolves had almost disappeared. More recently, as a few wolves migrated to northern Wisconsin forests, people continued to fear—and even to kill—them.

As their own feelings about wolves were changing, the Mead School fifth-graders realized that most people's negative feelings came from misinformation and from childhood fears. They learned about Wisconsin groups like the Timber Wolf Alliance, which works to change people's attitudes through education.

Then they heard that the Wisconsin Bureau of Endangered Resources was considering a plan to expand the wolf population to eighty in northern Wisconsin. They wondered how people there would react. They decided to find out. They created a questionnaire which asked people to respond (strongly agree, agree, no opinion, disagree or strongly disagree) to ten statements, from "It is a good idea to try and save the timber wolf," to "The only good wolf is a dead wolf!"

They sent 350 questionnaires to people chosen randomly in seventeen northern Wisconsin counties and enclosed a personal letter with every one. Sixty percent replied—an unusually high response. When they made graphs of the answers, they found that almost 75 percent were in favor of the timber wolf recovery plan.

The fifth-graders decided that the positive attitudes were partly due to work by the Timber Wolf Alliance, and they decided to support its activities. They made audio- and videocassettes of wolf songs and poems for the group to use. They made wolf tracks and wolf buttons to sell, and raised more than $100. Using information from their questionnaire, they also wrote letters to their state legislators supporting the wolf recovery plan.

Mead School friends of the timber wolf.

Then they started their own educational project with the younger children in their school. They read stories like "Little Red Riding Hood" aloud, let the children talk out their feelings and then taught them about real wolves. They hope these younger kids will grow up respecting wolves and looking forward to the day when Wisconsin has a stable wolf population once again.

PROJECTS

Good Eats

*A Two-Week Project That Can
Keep On Going*

It isn't easy to change people's eating habits—especially our own. Everyone has favorite foods and most people have some dislikes, too. We all tend to stick with familiar dishes instead of trying new ones. We may know we should eat low on the food chain for the good of the environment, but that doesn't mean we want to do it *tonight*. Or tomorrow, either. Maybe next year . . .

There are two sure ways to help yourself do something that seems hard: (1) Get other people to do it with you. (2) Make doing it enjoyable.

You probably know other people who would like to change the way they eat but aren't quite ready to start—kids in your class, scout group, church group or the people in your family. Ask them to start with you. "If you do it, I'll do it" is a good way to begin.

Set a goal. Make it realistic, something that everyone can easily do. Cooking one meatless meal for your family every week is an example. Be sure that everyone in your group agrees on the goal.

This project doesn't have to be dreary. Most people like to eat, and to fix things to eat. Most people eat meatless meals at least occasionally without even thinking about it. Now the point is to hunt for really good recipes that your family will like.

You can find them in books or in the newspaper, but the best way is to get them from other people. Ask the best cook you know for a recipe. Ask your friend. Ask your grandmother.

Cook, and eat, and discover which dishes your family likes best.

Your group could collect their favorites and put together a recipe booklet.

You could make booklets for everyone in your school to take home, or for the PTA to sell.

You could send sample recipes to the newspaper.

You could persuade your school cafeteria to serve one meatless dish every day. Offer them your recipes.

You could decide to eat meatless meals *twice* a week. You could get everyone in your group to do the same. You could get more people to join your group. You could keep going on and on. . . .

Getting Your Town to Compost

An Ongoing Project

Many towns recycle organic garbage (kitchen and garden waste) in compost piles and allow citizens to use the compost in their gardens.

Some advantages of composting are:

- It enriches the soil and helps plants grow.

- It saves money. Turning garbage into compost creates cheap fertilizer and saves the cost of dumping.

- It's better for the environment than chemical fertilizers.

- It saves landfill space. Solid waste could be reduced by 20 percent if all American garden waste were composted.

It's sensible for every town to compost organic garbage, but many towns still don't do it. The best way to convince your town to start composting is to build a demonstration compost pile.

If there's room for one in your schoolyard, how about making one as a class project? A schoolyard is a good place for a compost pile: many classes can work on it, and parents will see it. It can recycle cafeteria garbage, dead leaves and other outdoor material and reduce the school's trash load.

Many books give directions for starting a compost pile. You can find such a book in your library.

Make a plan. After you find out what materials you need, you may be able to get parents or local stores to donate them. When people feel connected to a project they're more likely to support it.

Keep records and take photographs as your class builds the compost bin and starts the compost pile. Write about it for the school paper and your local newspaper.

While the compost pile is working, do

some research on town composting. Find out how much landfill a town can save by composting kitchen and garden waste. Keep notes.

In four to eight weeks your first batch of compost should be ready. That would be a good time to present a composting proposal to your town government. Make an appointment to speak at a meeting. Choose a few people to represent the class. Take your notes and photos and a bag of your compost. Make sure that a newspaper reporter will be there.

If your town decides to compost, great. If it decides not to, you'll still have your school compost pile. You can't lose!

CHECKLIST

☐ When possible, buy fresh, unpackaged fruits and vegetables. Fruit that's in season is always fresher than out-of-season fruit, which has to be shipped a long distance.

☐ Peel wax-coated produce, like apples and cucumbers, before eating to remove as much pesticide as you can.

☐ Wash all fruits and vegetables well before you use them—soapy water is best—to get rid of the worst pesticide residue.

☐ If you have a garden, save seeds of the plants that you like best. Plant them in the spring or give them to friends.

☐ Build a birdhouse to put up near your home.

☐ Plant bushes with berries to attract birds to your yard. Birds help to control the insects that might otherwise eat your garden plants.

☐ Learn which garden plants are natural insect repellents for others, like marigolds for tomatoes.

☐ Decide to eat less meat. Get your friends to go out for pizza instead of hamburgers.

☐ Urge people not to release helium-filled balloons. When they fall to earth, fish, birds and other animals that eat them can become sick or die.

☐ Don't buy six-packs in plastic holders. They can entangle birds and animals.

☐ Join an organization that works for animals, like the Timber Wolf Alliance.

☐ Plant a tree near your house or ask your landlord, school, church or town government to plant one tree—or many. Trees cool buildings in summer and provide a nesting place for birds and animals.

HERE we are—more than five billion of us on the earth right now with 182 new babies being born every minute—heading toward the year 2000.

We face terrible problems. This book discusses many of them—global warming, acid rain, the ozone hole, deforestation, pollution of soil and water—and there are many more. Most of these problems are caused by human beings. But it's not useful to waste energy blaming ourselves or feeling guilty about the condition of the earth. We're not individually responsible for the population of the world, for the gap between the rich and poor nations, or for living in a country where each new baby puts a hundred times more stress on the world's resources than a baby born in a poorer country.

We *are* responsible for being aware of environmental problems and for understanding how our everyday actions affect them. Most of

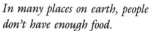

In many places on earth, people don't have enough food.

Automobiles change the landscape.

us would never think of poisoning our neighbors' drinking water. But we ought to know what happens if we pour a toxic cleaner down the drain—and what happens if our government exports toxic pesticides to farmers in developing countries.

Today we no longer have the excuse of ignorance or the luxury of indifference to environmental problems. We know that the earth is in danger and that it's up to ordinary people like us to preserve it. This is something new in history.

At the end of the last century, when machines to produce consumer goods were invented and factories began to pollute the air and the land, most people simply accepted pollution as the price of what seemed to be progress. Machine-made products like cloth and china and farm tools made ordinary people's lives far easier than ever before. Producing and selling these wonderful new products made other people rich. Few people considered the human and environmental costs of industrial development. The machine age had begun.

A generation later, after the automobile had been invented and mass production made buying a car possible for many people in the United States, few stopped to think about the vast impact cars and road-building would have on the environment. And some who did think about it did not care, like the car makers who realized that the network of trolleys that ran between many small country towns might

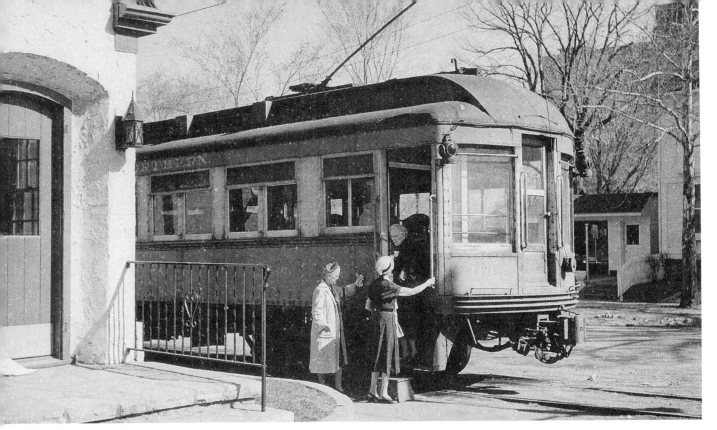

An interurban trolley.

compete with future car sales. These businessmen bought the land the trolleys crossed, tore up the rails and destroyed a cheap, convenient and non-polluting way to travel.

As recently as fifty years ago, after cars had become common, people still didn't realize how drastically their use would change the land and the atmosphere, the design of cities and the arrangement of work and personal life in industrial countries. No one predicted traffic jams, shopping malls, two-hour commutes or a death rate from car accidents equal to that from war. No one anticipated devastating oil spills, the possibility of warfare over oil resources, or the threat of global warming.

Although many people now understand the effect cars have on the environment, it's still enormously difficult to change a way of life based on the automobile. Car makers resist converting their factories to the production of small, high-mileage cars. Oil companies resist government regulations on drilling and tanker design. Politicians resist passing laws promoting clean air or reducing highway speeds. Advertisers resist selling fuel economy and safety and talk more about luxury and speed. And most car owners themselves resist cutting back on car use. So the land is paved over with highways and shopping centers, the atmosphere is fouled with car emissions, and neighborhoods decay as people use up time and energy traveling far from home to work and shop.

It's clear that to preserve the environment we must reduce our reliance on automobiles and support other ways—like mass transportation, car pools, bike riding and walking—of getting from one place to another.

Riding in cars is only one of many habits we'll need to change in the 1990s. We'll need to figure out how to recycle seriously—not just sorting out bottles into separate bins, but inventing ways to use all the earth's resources without using them up as carelessly as we do now. Old-growth forests, rain forests, fossil fuels, clean water and fertile soil are all running out, and the needs of a growing world population will deplete them even faster. We'll have to understand that natural resources are part of the world's wealth, and that using them up will make us and our children poorer.

It is the job of the people now on earth to achieve a sustainable society, to meet our own needs without using up resources that future generations are going to need. We will have to shift to renewable energy resources like solar energy instead of fossil fuels; we'll have to design factories that make paper and glass and aluminum from recycled materials; we'll have to plant new forests, eat less meat, cut back on wasteful packaging, make homes and public buildings weathertight, and use organic garbage and treated sewage as fertilizer for crops. We'll need to elect governments that cut back on military spending and spend that money on improving the environment. We'll need to plan for job conversion so that workers in fields like mining, logging

Subways transport huge numbers of people without creating traffic jams or pollution.

and weapons production will get job training and help in finding new jobs in occupations like forestry, solar and wind energy, housing, mass transportation and the repair and recycling of goods.

To create a truly sustainable society, we will have to face up to the problem of population. Earth's resources are limited, but the number of people on earth is growing rapidly. At the present rate, the population will double by the middle of the next century. The earth cannot sustain that many people. If we don't reduce the birthrate, we condemn future generations to death from hunger and malnutrition. It's our responsibility to understand the relationship between family size and sustainability, and to plan to have small families.

People in the 1990s must resolve to reduce inequality. We cannot truly think globally unless we understand the enormous differences in the way people live today. At the moment you are reading this, 80 percent of all people alive live in poverty. You've seen pictures of hungry and homeless people in far-off countries and in our own country as well. Poor people lack the basic necessities and comforts that the 20 percent who are well-off take for granted. The environment of the poor is more polluted, they have less opportunity for good education, and their health is not as good. Everyone has a right to food, shelter, health and peace, but the majority of people now alive do not have these things.

To reach equality, these people—most of them in developing countries—may need assistance from richer nations to achieve an improved standard of living. But aid will have to come from sustainable energy resources instead of from the fossil fuels that developed nations have relied on in the past. Our mistakes are clear and we don't want other countries to repeat them. Any assistance we give them should fit their needs—not our idea of what they need. Of course, we must stop exporting dangerous products, like pesticides and cigarettes, to other countries. Ordinary citizens have to keep check on their governments and protest such harmful actions anywhere in the world.

Meanwhile, people in the richest countries need to cut down on what they consume. We don't need everything that's advertised on TV. We don't need to eat a hamburger every night or to buy clothes we'll only wear a few times. We don't really need to use polystyrene cups or paper napkins or to buy products wrapped in layers of plastic. We don't have to throw anything usable away—we can give it to a friend, sell it at a garage sale or donate it to a thrift shop.

An old rhyme goes:

Use it up,
Wear it out,
Make it do
Or do without.

Neighborhood recycling.

A hundred years ago, it would have shocked most people to throw away anything usable. Now we live in a throwaway society. It's not our fault that we were born into it, but we don't have to keep old habits. We can change.

People do change. Many people once thought smoking was sophisticated. Rich, elegant people in the movies and smart-looking people in magazine ads smoked cigarettes. Kids used to think smoking meant being grown up. Then we began to learn that smoking causes lung cancer and other diseases. More and more people—many of them doctors—explained the horrible effects of smoking. Magazines showed pictures of lung cancer victims. It took many years before warning messages were required on cigarette packages and cigarette advertisements, and it took even longer before smoking was banned in workplaces, theaters and airplanes. Today there is a decrease in the number of smokers in the United States. A few people still think it is sophisticated to smoke, but many more think it is stupid and dangerous. People's attitudes *do* change.

While fewer people smoke now than in previous decades, it will still take many years to change United States farm policies that support tobacco raising; to restore the land to productive use; to reverse trade policies that allow for the export of cigarettes to other countries;

Bicycles are inexpensive, convenient and non-polluting.

to pay for the health costs of those who continue to smoke; to educate new generations about the dangers of smoking and to achieve a truly smoke-free society.

People and governments can change in other ways. For nearly fifty years of this century, most citizens of the United States and the Soviet Union believed their nations would be enemies forever. Both countries tried to protect themselves by building huge stockpiles of nuclear weapons. Today, the United States and the Soviet Union are no longer enemies—striking evidence that attitudes do change. But the stockpiles of nuclear weapons built up in earlier days are only slowly being reduced, while the hazardous waste of years of nuclear-weapon production continues to seep into the land.

Today, people around the world are aware that the environment is in danger. We know we must change our attitudes and our behavior—and influence our governments to change—in order to save our earth. We know that change is possible and that we have to begin now.

Although human beings share the earth with millions of other species, ours is the only one that can remember its history and plan for its future. Unlike other species, we have the language, tools and art to understand our environment. We have the intelligence and courage to take care of it. We have each other to support and work with. We have hope.

■ Ten thousand years ago, there were probably about five million people in the entire world—fewer people than live in New York City today.

- In 1987, the world's population passed five billion.
- If present rates of population growth continue, world population will pass ten billion soon after the turn of the next century.

■ There are 157 billionaires in the world today.

- There are probably two million millionaires in the world today.
- There are 100 million homeless people in the world today.

■ Women grow 60 percent of the world's food; they own 1 percent of the world's property.

■ It would cost each human being on earth $1 apiece to save 14 million children who die each year from treatable diseases such as diarrhea.

■ The cost of one Stealth Bomber is $530 million.

■ Every day 40,000 of the world's poorest children under age five die unnecessarily for lack of basic health care and medicine.

■ There are one and a quarter soldiers for every one inhabitant of the developing world. There is one doctor for every 1,950 inhabitants of the developing world.

■ The world grows less grain than it eats, and is using up its stocks.

■ Every day, the average American uses 168 gallons of water.

■ There are 1.8 billion people in the developing world (excluding China) without access to fresh water.

■ To collect and recycle paper provides five times as many jobs as to harvest virgin timber.

■ In 1981, 45 percent of Americans polled agreed that protecting the environment is so important that improvements must be made regardless of the cost. In 1990, 74 percent of Americans agreed with that statement.

People everywhere are working to save the earth. They're planting gardens, clearing park land, recycling, working to provide affordable, energy-efficient housing, planting trees. You can join them.

City Volunteer Corps.

Tree People.

The Student Conservation Association, Inc.

Habitat for Humanity.

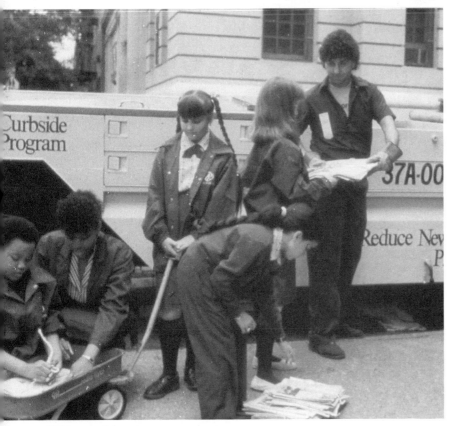

Girl Scouts of America.

Tree People.

People and Space

A Thirty-Minute Project

There is only so much space on earth.

There will never be more than there is now—and each bit of land that becomes unlivable makes the total less.

But the numbers of people on earth keep growing. At some point, the earth will not be able to support them all. There will not be enough food, water or space to go around.

The only way to have a smaller population on earth is for people to have fewer children, and for those children to have

fewer children, and so on for generations.

You can get a quick picture of the difference between having three children and having two children in a few generations of a family by making the following diagrams.

Take two pieces of typing paper (8½″ × 11″). Turn them sideways. This will be the space for diagraming your descendants. Draw seven lines about an inch apart across each page.

Draw a small circle above the center of the top line of both pages. This is you.

On the two-child diagram, draw two circles with space between them on the top line. These will stand for the two children you might have. On the three-child diagram, draw three separated circles on the top line to stand for *three* children.

Now assume your two children each have two children of their own. Draw lines from their circles to the next horizontal line

and put two circles there for each, to stand for your grandchildren. Assume your three children each have *three* children, and draw lines to circles that represent them.

Keep adding two circles for each child on the two-child diagram and three circles for each on the three-child diagram, to stand for your descendants. Go all the way to the seventh line, if you can.

Now you can begin to see the difference it would make, in just one family, if each generation had three children instead of two.

Your diagram is only about numbers. It doesn't show you how real people will act in the future, or what their real lives will be like. We can't predict all the problems of overpopulation—and we can't predict ways that people will invent to cope with these problems. Thinking about the numbers is only the first step.

Ad Alert

An Ongoing Project

After you've learned some facts about the environment, some advertisements may surprise you.

You may wonder how a diaper company can boast about "biodegradable diapers" when you know they won't degrade in a landfill for decades. You may wonder how an oil company can write about saving wildlife when you know that oil drilling pollutes the environment.

Naturally, no company wants people to think it pollutes or damages the environment. Some companies would rather spend money on confusing, untruthful ads than

pay the costs of avoiding or cleaning up pollution.

Don't let them fool you. When you read an ad you don't believe, tear it out. When you hear one on TV, write it down. Save the ads. Try to discover the facts behind a company's claims and tape your notes to the back of the ad.

Write letters to the companies. Save the answers you get.

A collection of ads with your corrections to them and letters about them would be a valuable addition to your school library.

A Catalog of Stupid Things

A Now-and-Then Project

There's a lot of junk for sale that no one really needs. It takes energy to sell this stuff: to think it up, wrap it up, transport it, advertise it and sell it. It takes energy to get rid of it, too: to throw it out, pick it up, sort it, transport it and dump it.

You can't keep people from making stupid things. But you might get a few people to consider not buying them if you make a "Catalog of Stupid Things."

Buy a notebook, or make one by stapling scrap paper together.

Look for the most ridiculous advertisements you can find in old newspapers, magazines and catalogs—ads for stuff you and your friends would laugh at.

Cut out the ads and tape them into the notebook.

When all the pages are filled, you have your "Catalog of Stupid Things."

Show it to people. They'll probably laugh at it. They might remember it the next time they start to buy something they don't need.

War Games/War Toys

Two Saturday Projects

You know that wars kill people and ruin the environment. But you've probably noticed that a lot of programs for children make war and killing seem exciting, and try to get kids to buy war toys.

How much fighting is there on TV for young children? You can find out with a survey.

Decide what you want to count, whether it's the number of times two people fight, the number of people who get killed, or the number of battles or bombings or space wars. Decide whether you're going to look at just one channel, or switch around the dial every half-hour.

Draw lines on a piece of paper to show times and channels, with space for your check marks.

Pick a Saturday, get up early, turn on the TV and start counting.

Be sure to write down the name of each program. You may want to add notes on which ones you think are boring or interesting or scary to little kids.

At noon, turn off the TV.

Later, you could interview some young children. Which programs do they like? Which ones do they think are dumb?

Your research could make an interesting report. You could use it in a letter to the newspaper, or to the sponsor of one of the shows you watched.

You can do the same kind of research on ads for war toys by counting the number advertised on any Saturday morning and describing the ads you saw.

You could interview some little kids about the ads to find out which toys they want most.

You could follow up this project with research in a toy store. Compare the space given to war toys to the amount of space given to all other kinds of toys.

There are groups that encourage shoppers not to buy war toys for children. At holiday times they stand outside toy stores and urge shoppers to buy peaceful toys. You might decide to join such a group.

People Around the World

A Fifteen-Minute Project

If all the people on earth today held hands in a continuous line, how many times would the line go around the world?

To get an answer, all you need are another person, a ruler and these three facts:

1. There are approximately five billion people in the world today.

2. The circumference of the earth is approximately 25,000 miles.

3. When you stand next to another person and hold hands, the distance between your noses is _____.

☐ Read the newspaper. Keep up with environmental news.

☐ Read books and magazines about the environment.

☐ Watch TV programs about the environment.

☐ Ask questions. Check your facts with several sources. Learn the background of issues as well as the facts. Don't believe everything you read, see or hear.

☐ Talk about environmental issues with your family, your friends, your neighbors, your class.

☐ Pay attention to the connections between what you do and what you're doing to the environment.

☐ Resolve to change some things you do in order to improve the environment. Make the easy changes quickly.

☐ Give people gifts that help the environment, like garden tools or flower boxes or memberships in environmental organizations.

☐ Resolve to consider the environment when you plan your life. Start to think about the work you want to do, the way you want to live, the kind of family you want to have. Think about how many trees you hope to plant during your lifetime.

☐ Plant a tree, or many trees. A tree's green beauty and cool shade will give pleasure to many people for years to come.

KAP Presents...

ENVIRONMENTAL DAY

GETTING TO WORK

You'll be amazed at how much you can find out in a library. You can learn just about everything you need to know.

You can do research in most libraries whether or not you have a card. But you'll need a card to take out books.

Don't be afraid to ask librarians for help. They won't do your research for you, but they can show you how to find the information you need. As an example, let's say you want to learn all you can about the *Exxon Valdez* oil spill in Alaska.

You'd like to read a newspaper article written right after the *Valdez* spill happened. But you don't know what the date was.

Find out if your library has the *New York Times* and the *New York Times Index* available on microfilm. If they don't, they can tell you where to find it in some other library or help you find another index of newspaper articles. Ask the librarian to help you learn how to use the *Index*.

You'd like to learn more about oil spills in general, maybe read a whole book about them.

Check the card or computer catalog. Start with "oil spills," then think of other possible subject headings, like "environment" and "energy." Even if there's no whole book on the topic, you might find several books with chapters about it.

You'd like to find out more about the *Valdez* spill, but there's no book about it.

Look it up in the *Reader's Guide to Periodical Literature.* (Ask the librarian where to find it.) This index lists thousands of magazine articles according to their subject. See what you can find by looking up several different subjects, like "oil spills—animals" or "*Exxon Valdez—*trial." If the *Guide* lists an article in *Newsweek* magazine that looks interesting, ask the librarian where the magazine files are kept. If the library doesn't have that issue of *Newsweek,* they may be able to get it for you from another library.

You've found a listing for a good book on the topic, but it's not in your library.

You can probably receive the book through interlibrary loan. Your library will contact other libraries in your area. If one of them owns the book, the librarian can borrow it from them. (This procedure may take time.)

You want to know the names of groups that clean up/monitor/lobby against oil spills.

You'll find such groups listed in the *Encyclopedia of Associations,* a reference book that can be found in most public libraries. Ask your librarian where it is. There are organizations that deal with just about everything you could imagine. This book gives a little information about each one as well as their addresses and phone numbers.

You want to write a letter to the president of Exxon. How can you find his or her name and address?

There are several directories that list businesses and give the names of their chief executive officers. Ask your librarian for *Standard & Poor's Register, Moody's* or *Dun and Bradstreet.*

You want to learn more about Alaska.

Look it up in the encyclopedia. If your library has several different sets, look it up in each one. Different encyclopedias give different kinds of information.

What's the exact population of Alaska?

Look it up in the *World Almanac.* This is a great source of all kinds of information, including news events (it may have some information on the oil spill). The *Almanac* includes a section on the environment, where you can find information on endangered species, oil pipelines, oil prices and related topics.

You want to write to your senator and Congressional representative but don't know their names. You would also like to know the name of the senator from Alaska.

Ask to see the *Official Congressional Directory*.

When Andrew Holleman decided to fight the development of a wetland site near his home, he needed information. He had to find out what Massachusetts law says about protecting wetlands, and he had to study his town's master plan to see how the site was zoned. He found copies of the law and of the master plan at his local library.

JOIN IN

With Environmental Groups

There are hundreds of environmental groups in the United States. Almost all of them, with addresses and phone numbers, are listed in the *Encyclopedia of Associations,* which you can find in most libraries.

These organizations will answer questions, help you find a local group near you and send you materials about their work.

To find out what groups near you are doing, read the newspapers and watch for notices of meetings.

To see if there are community groups you don't know about, look under "Environmental" in the Yellow Pages.

Most groups have open meetings that anyone can attend and projects that anyone can help with. These groups are usually glad to have kids work with them.

Hi. This is Amy Tanaka, in Arlington, and I'm calling because my class wants to know if you need volunteers for the Clean River Project. . . .

With Your Family

People sometimes say that saving the environment begins at home. It's true that small changes in everyone's home can add up to giant improvements in the environment. But beginning at home may not be as easy as it sounds. Families don't always act the way you want them to or the way books say they will. You can't *make* your mom stop buying paper towels; you can't *make* your sister walk instead of beg to be driven somewhere.

But you can influence your family to change.

Tell Them

Share what you know about the environment—not just the bad news, but the good news, too. It can get discouraging to hear about one more chemical that poisons the environment, but it's great to hear how scientists are saving wild species, like the trumpeter swan, from extinction. Talk about facts you read in the paper, or an organization you learned about at school, or a TV show you saw at a friend's house.

Show Them

Start making changes yourself. Get in the habit of using a sponge to clean up with, instead of a paper towel. Try walking when you want to go somewhere. Set an example for your family.

Bargain with Them

Say you'll help unpack the groceries, if they'll reuse the bags the next time they shop. Offer to return the bottles if they'll stop tossing them in the trash. Say you'll do the dishes more often if you can use soap instead of a polluting detergent.

Convince Them

At Schroeder School in Huntington Beach, California, sixth-grader Trieu Duong wrote this article for a parents' newsletter:

Adults need to go back to school and learn the three R's again. . . . No, they are not reading, 'riting and 'rithmetic; they are recycle, reuse and reduce.

First, there's recycle. This is the process of turning used things into new materials. For example, plastic bottles could be recycled and turned to new things such as carpeting and fiberfill to make ski jackets and sleeping bags.

Next, there's reuse. This is the process of using materials over and over before recycling them. For instance, you could use two-liter soft-drink bottles for arts-and-crafts projects.

And last, but definitely not least . . . there's reduce. To reduce is to buy the smallest amount of containers possible. The result: less amount of waste to throw away!

This is all I have to say, but you parents shouldn't just *read* about saving the earth, you should *do* it, too.

In Your Neighborhood

Neighbors can do a lot to improve their own environment. But first they have to organize. You and your friends could help start a neighborhood association.

Talk about it at home. Talk to the neighbors. Ask *them* to talk about it.

Offer to publicize a meeting.

People around the country are doing this. They're getting together to plant trees in front of their houses, make gardens in their back yards, protest noise pollution, fight toxic waste and resist unplanned development in their neighborhoods. You can't do these things alone, but you and your friends and family and neighbors can start to do them together.

At School

Get your class to take a serious look at your school's environment.

- What can you learn from the land right around your school—the playground or parking area or cement walks? Are there ways to make this space more usable?
- Where does your school get the food for lunches? What can you do to reduce food waste?
- How could you convince your school cafeteria to serve less beef and to buy local fruits and vegetables?
- How could your school save energy? Water?
- What about noise pollution?

Some questions to ask before you start:

- Which school authorities will you need to convince?
- What facts will you need to show them?
- What volunteer work will need to be done?
- How much free time are you willing to give?
- Can you get some other classes to work with you?

With Kids Around the Country

When you begin to work for the environment, you'll start to notice that other kids are doing it, too. You'll read articles about them or hear about them on TV.

Get in touch! They can give you good ideas. You can give them some of yours. Here are ways to reach them:

· Write a letter.

Hi! We're doing a project that's sort of like yours, except the stream we're working on is in the city. So far, we did four Saturday cleanups. We collected two truckloads of trash! We were on the news on TV. If you want, we can send you a videocassette. We read about you in a magazine. How did you get the mayor and all those people to help you?

· Call up. If you don't know the number of the group you want to reach, find the area code of their city on the map in your phone book. Dial the area code plus 555-1212, for Directory Assistance.

· A good way to learn about other kids' groups is through an organization called Renew America. This group keeps a record of successful environmental projects around the country. It's called the *Environmental Success Index,* and it lists a lot of kids' projects, with their addresses and phone numbers. You can nominate your own project for the *Success Index!* For information on how to do it, write or call Renew America. (See page 114).

SPEAK OUT

When you know enough and care enough about an environmental problem, you'll want to tell other people how you feel. There are lots of ways to do it. Don't worry that people won't listen because you're a kid. That can be an advantage. People are supposed to care about kids. Most people really do, and those who don't wouldn't want to admit it.

Say what you think. You have the power to make people listen.

Write Letters

You can write to anyone—to the mayor of your town, to the head of a company or a TV station, to the editor of your newspaper, to the governor of your state or to a member of Congress. You can write to the President of the United States.

Ms. Susan Greening, Mayor
City Hall
Middletown, U.S.A.

Dear Mayor Greening:

Our class at Inwood School has been studying waste. We learned that polystyrene produces toxins when you make it and when you throw it away. Plus, it's hard to recycle, and it takes up space in landfills. It is an unnecessary product and it is not good for our town.

We believe our town should ban polystyrene the way a lot of other cities do, including Portland, Oregon, Minneapolis and St. Paul, Minnesota, and Newark, New Jersey. We are enclosing an article about how they banned it.

Please write back.

Sincerely,
Brian Engle, for Class 6-2

Support your facts with examples. Always ask for an answer.

Dear Brian and Class 6-2:

Thank you for your letter about polystyrene. I have passed it on to the Waste Management Committee of the Town Council. A proposal to ban polystyrene products would have to be brought to the Town Council.

Sincerely,
Susan Greening, Mayor

Don't let someone put you off. Keep writing.

Charles Mackey
Waste Management Committee
Middletown Town Council

Dear Councilman Mackey:

    Mayor Greening has written our class that she gave you our letter about banning polystyrene. We hope you and other members of the Waste Management Committee will bring this question up at a meeting of the Town Council. When you do, we would like to make a presentation.
    Please reply.

Sincerely,
Brian Engle, Class 6-2

Copy to members of Waste Management Committee
Copy to Mayor Greening

Tell people who else you're writing to. Follow up on their replies.

Mr. William Johnston
House of Representatives
Washington, D.C. 20516

Dear Mr. Johnston:

I am writing to ask you to help to stop the United States Forest Service from selling timber in our national forests at low prices to companies that make paper from new pulp. Because the prices are so low, these companies can sell new paper cheaper than companies that make paper from recycled pulp.

If people cannot afford to make and buy recycled paper, then what will happen to all the newspaper that is collected for recycling? It will just fill up our landfills.

Recycled paper ought to cost less, not more! Do you know that every ton of recycled paper saves seventeen trees? We should save the national forests, not cut them down.

Please reply. I will use your answer in my school report on recycling.

LaVerne DeSantis

Let Congressional representatives know that you'll tell others what they say. Get others to write, too. A letter-writing campaign can influence a vote.

The President of the United States
The White House
1600 Pennsylvania Avenue N.W.
Washington, D.C. 20500

Dear Mr. President:

I am a seventh-grade student at Landis Middle School. Our class has been studying environmental issues. To me, the most important issue of all is nuclear weapons, because nuclear war could destroy the whole environment of our planet. I am glad we are starting to reduce our stockpile of nuclear weapons. But I think we should get rid of them all. We don't need them.

There is also a health risk involved in producing nuclear weapons. When the nuclear plant in the Soviet Union called Chernobyl broke down, many people near it died, others lost their homes, and food was contaminated all over Northern Europe. Also, producing nuclear weapons creates toxic waste and there is no way to get rid of it. Nobody wants nuclear waste in their back yard.

I think we should take the money we spend on nuclear weapons and use it to clean up the environment. That would make the world safer *and* better for all people to live in.

Sincerely,
Greg Goldman

One person alone may not influence the President. But letters from many people may help to convince him. Send a copy of the letter to your newspaper.

To the Editor, *Springfield News Leader:*

I have sent the enclosed letter to the President of the United States. I hope that other people in Springfield who feel the way I do will write to him, too. I think everyone should tell the President that we don't want nuclear weapons.

Sincerely,
Greg Goldman

Make a Speech

Members of Kids Against Pollution in Closter, New Jersey, have flown to many parts of the country to give talks about their work. They explain how they started their group in Mr. Byrne's fifth-grade class and how KAP has expanded to a network of 500 groups around the United States and in five foreign countries. The original KAP members are used to giving speeches by now, and they do it well. But some adults aren't too eager to listen to them—at first.

KAP members speak at an Environmental Rights Day program.

Here's what Kate Malmrose of KAP said about a recent speech:

I had to get up at 4:30 A.M. to go with my teacher to Newark Airport for a 7:00 A.M. flight. We arrived at Columbia, South Carolina, at 11:00 A.M., went to the conference and then to a banquet lunch. I was the only kid there, so at first the adults gave me the brush. Two people spoke before me. When I got up some people left, probably thinking my speech would be stupid. (They apologized later!)

I spoke with confidence and I got through the twelve pages. The next thing I knew the people were giving me a standing ovation and giving me all kinds of compliments. It was really an exciting day.

Make Audiotapes or Videotapes

A tape or video recording is a good way to keep a record, prove a point or publicize your work. You can send tapes to other people or groups to show them what you're doing, and you can send them to your local radio and television stations. If you or your group doesn't have a tape recorder or a video camera, see if you can borrow one from your school or library.

This is Bill Hood, at the edge of Tallman Marsh on Sunday morning, May 25, on a bird-watching hike with the Rockland Audubon Society. What you hear in the background is the song of the red-winged blackbirds all around us. You can also hear some ducks quacking. Hey—here come two Canada geese flying over, just in time to get on the tape!

This is Joy, with Robert and Lydia. We're in Mr. Rich's sixth grade, and we're making this tape for our school environment project. We're standing in the back of the Kennedy School cafeteria at 12:15 P.M. on Tuesday, October 1. About 120 kids are in the cafeteria now. The noise you hear is dishes and silverware and trays clattering and people yelling and benches getting pulled out and stuff like that. If it's hard for you to hear me, well, then you get the idea of what a normal lunch period at Kennedy is like.

Good afternoon. I'm Kalim Jackson, president of the eighth grade at Newton Middle School, which is the sponsor of this meeting on reducing energy use at Newton. I would like to welcome our guests, Principal Clarence Stoddard; Mr. Arlo Smith, the school custodian; and Mr. John O'Reilly, an engineer who's the father of Sam O'Reilly in our class. Thanks to you all for coming. Now we would like to present our research on this topic, and ask each of you to comment on it. . . .

Troop 5, Boy Scouts of America of Annandale, Illinois, presents: *Making a Nature Walk for Annandale*.

The project began one year ago. Here we are, with our troop leader Mr. Short, making a map of the area. All through the year, we documented our progress—and our hard work—on videotape.

Now that the nature walk is finished, it's hard to remember what the land looked like when we began.

But there it is: Palmer Meadow, a five-acre field behind the Colonial Mall on Route 300, before we started to work.

Pretty much of a jungle, right, guys? A lot of thorns in there. And look out for that poison ivy! . . .

■

Kite Day—A celebration of spring at Murphy School: 205 kids, 205 kites in the air!

This video was made by Southeast High School Video Productions, with the cooperation of students and faculty at Murphy School, and with special thanks to the fifth grade. Fifth-grader Julie Novak explains the history of Kite Day:

Kite Day is something new. We used to have Balloon Day every May 1. Every kid in the school got a balloon, and we put messages on them and let them go in the air. Sometimes we got a message back.

But this year, our class learned that when the balloons came down they were a danger to birds and animals who got caught in them. What to do about Balloon Day?

Someone said, how about having Kite Day, instead?

So we started to make kites. . . .

Sixth graders from the Main Street Middle School hold a press conference.

Hold a Press Conference

When you have important news that you want everyone to hear, call a press conference. Invite reporters from local newspapers and radio and television stations. Inviting well-known people, like the governor of your state, the mayor of your town or your Congressional representative makes it more likely that reporters will show up. Your presentation should be carefully planned, brief and interesting.

Sixth-graders at Main Street Middle School, in Montpelier, Vermont, held a press conference at City Hall when they published their report on their yearlong Food Works project on hunger and food policy in their city.

At the press conference, they cited problems of malnutrition and increased demands on the city's food pantry, told of planting their own school gardens, explained their plan for 300 gardens within the city and a fruit tree in every yard and discussed their vision of Montpelier as a "garden city" in the year 2000.

In addition, they presented their food policy survey, to which they asked citizens to respond.

Articles about the press conference appeared in newspapers throughout Vermont. It was covered on radio and TV, and Vermont senator Patrick Leahy entered a report of the project in the *Congressional Record*.

Congressional Record

United States of America

PROCEEDINGS AND DEBATES OF THE 100th CONGRESS, SECOND SESSION

Vol. 134   WASHINGTON, MONDAY, JUNE 6, 1988   No. 81

Senate

THE MONTPELIER FOOD POLICY PROJECT BY THE MAIN STREET MIDDLE SCHOOL

Mr. LEAHY. Mr. President, Kristin Commito, a sixth grade student from Montpelier, came into my Vermont office this week to give me a booklet entitled "The Montpelier Food Policy—A Project by the Sixth Grade Class of the Main Street Middle School, Montpelier, VT, 1988." She was proud of the project that her class had just completed. And after reading the booklet, I was proud, too.

The sixth graders of the Main Street Middle School tackled a job that I have been working on for years in the Senate Agriculture Committee— hunger and malnutrition. They recognized that hunger is not just a problem in Third World countries but that it also hits Montpelier, VT. They not only recognized the problem, but decided to do something about it.

They divided the six grade classes into committees: needs, education and promotion, food enterprise, land mapping, and action. These committees formulated game plans to raise public awareness of hunger in Montpelier and to call attention to the insufficiency of Federal, State, and local assistance to hungry families.

Nutrition education can help people understand proper nutrition, while classes in gardening can help Vermonters grow their own nutritious foods to help meet their needs. Food enterprise can establish projects that make money and create jobs for Vermonters through plant sales, bottle drives, community canning or freezing plants, farmers markets, and so forth. The money can be donated to the Montpelier Food Pantry and the Vermont Food Bank and can help establish community garden plots and publish pamphlets on hunger.

Land mapping could help convert open land in Montpelier to land used for planting and growing food.

Mr. President, I will ask that the introduction to the booklet be printed in the RECORD following my remarks.

The six graders at the Main Street Middle School not only see that hunger is a real problem but have taken action to help alleviate it. They are now talking with the mayor, the planning commission, and the city council in order to make their Montpelier Food Policy an alternative for the future.

I am proud of these students and I hope that their project becomes a reality.

I ask that the introduction to the booklet be printed in the RECORD.

The introduction follows:

THE MONTPELIER FOOD POLICY—A PROJECT BY THE SIXTH GRADE CLASS OF THE MAIN STREET MIDDLE SCHOOL, MONTPELIER, VT, 1988

INTRODUCTION

The sixth graders of Main Street Middle School were upset when we discovered, by visiting the food pantry, how much malnutrition there is in our community.

Many middle and working poor class families need Emergency Food to get by. There are several (high expenses) that need to get paid each month such as mortgage, rent, electric, and utility bills, and, if these bills are not paid, serious consequences like eviction may occur. However, there is one bill that may be cut back—food.

By the end of a month, Food Stamps, which supplement every meal and help many families make ends meet, run out. People who are faced with this problem every month need to find another way to get food, and many resort to the Montpelier Emergency Food Pantry, thus the pantry is used heavily and often runs short of food to distribute.

We wanted to help find the solution to this problem, and we started by writing letters and developing this policy, because we want more control over our food (how it is grown the use of herbicides, pesticides and fungicides, etc.) and we would like to help the hunger situation. We don't have any solution for this problem, but we have opened the gateway to the answer.

CHILDREN SPEAKING OUT

Many people say we are just children and we should wait until we are older to create anything like this.

However, we are the next generation. It's our own future, and if we analyze the malnutrition problem now, we'll have the answer well under way soon.

There are so many possibilities! How do you pick one?

Choose something you really care about.
That's the first step.

Start small.
Pick a realistic goal—one that you know your group can reach. It's discouraging to start out on a project that overwhelms you, even if it's really worthwhile. A big project, like creating a wildlife preserve at the edge of your town, could easily take a year of planning, meetings, money-raising and weekend work. That's not a good project for beginners.

Expect to learn more than you expected.
You'll learn a lot from working on a simple project—for example, putting up bat houses around your school.
You'll learn how to choose a project, how to plan it and how to keep records of your work.
Next, you'll learn how to find information about bats, those fascinating flying mammals.

You'll discover that a bat house containing 50 bats could eat up to 30 million insects in a summer.

You'll learn about your school's natural environment, about the temperature of brick, about carpentry (if you build the bat houses) or about money-raising (if you buy them).

You'll learn about working with people. You'll probably find that everyone works better when the task and the goals are clear. You may find that it's good to set short-term goals and to check your progress as you go along.

You may learn some school rules you didn't know before. You'll probably get to know your principal and custodian better. You may learn how to get other students—even the youngest ones—interested in what you're doing and ready to help you keep the project going.

You'll probably discover that most people don't know much about bats, and that many people are scared of them. You may learn enough to teach them something!

Even if no bats nest in your houses this year, you will end up with some good experience for starting the next project.

Some Sample Projects

- Locate a company that sells string bags at a good price. Order a large quantity to sell outside your local supermarket. Use your profits to finance new projects.

- Prepare a questionnaire about pesticides for produce managers of grocery stores near you. Tabulate and publicize the results.

- Make an environmental map of your school playground, showing plant and animal life. Ask if you can take the first-graders in your school on a nature walk around the playground.

- Research and prepare a fact sheet on plastic containers. Send a committee to present it to managers of fast-food restaurants where kids in your school eat. Ask the restaurant managers about their plans for reducing use of plastic. Decide on your plans for consumer action.

- Write a proposal to make your town a nuclear-free zone. Get endorsements from community leaders. Present the proposal to your city government.

- Convince your school's PTA to sponsor planting a tree in the schoolyard to honor every retiring teacher and staff member. Research the best type of tree for your school environment. If someone is retiring this year, take charge of selecting and planting the tree, and publicizing the ceremony.

Think About It

Saving the earth takes work—volunteer work and work for pay. Many people now make their living at jobs that improve the environment—they're scientists, writers, farmers, organizers and people in business and government.

In the future, when you're ready to start work, there will be even more environmental jobs. Industries like logging, defense, automobile production and oil exploration may cut back on the number of workers they employ. But there will be many new jobs in housing, construction, agriculture, alternative energy, community planning and human services.

Learn About It

If you want an environmental career, you can begin to plan for it right now. Two good ways to find out about jobs are to read about them and to ask people who have them.

You'll find books, magazine articles and pamphlets about careers in your library. A helpful book that describes a variety of jobs is *A Complete Guide to Environmental Careers.*

You can learn even more about environmental work by talking to somebody who does it for a living: a recycling engineer, a park supervisor, a town planner, a biologist, an organic farmer, an environmental lawyer. Most people really like to talk about their work and might be willing to meet with you. Call them up.

When you reach them, you may feel shy, but remember: they can't see you; they don't know if you have notes in front of you. It's a good idea to have notes. They help you remember the questions you want to ask and they make you sound smart.

RECEPTIONIST: Good morning . . . Solar Power Industries.
BLOCK: Mr. Jack Watkins, please, in the research department.

(Ring, ring, ring.)

WATKINS: Watkins speaking.
BLOCK: Hi. This is Kevin Block. I read about you in an article in *Scientific American*. I wanted to ask you if you might have a summer job for me with your solar-power project. Is this a good time to talk?
WATKINS: Well, actually, I'm pretty busy right now. Could you call back?
BLOCK: Sure. When would be a good time?
WATKINS: How about, say, around ten tomorrow?
BLOCK: (Oh, man, that's math class. Well, I'll just have to explain to Mrs. Brice. She'll probably let me make the call.) Sure. That's fine. I'll call you then. Kevin Block's my name.
WATKINS: Okay. Talk to you tomorrow.

Do It

If you decide you want to work for the environment, it's never too early to start. Any work that you do, whether you're paid for it or not, is good experience. Employers are always looking for people with experience.

Talk about your job interests with your family, your teachers, your guidance counselor and anyone you think can help you.

Organize volunteer projects at your school.

Look for summer jobs in fields that interest you.

Work with community organizations.

Use the library. Know what's going on, locally and around the world.

Take classes that will give you the background for the kind of job you want. Don't limit yourself to science classes: a journalism class can teach you how to write clearly on environmental topics; a sociology class can teach you how people's attitudes change; a history class can teach you how agricultural discoveries have affected world hunger.

Learn about colleges with environmental programs. Write to them for information.

Think about the kind of work that will need to be done in the next century. Think about the kind of work you would like to do.

Jay Holcomb and Dory Kistner-Morris have each made working for the environment a career.

Two Environmentalists

Jay Holcomb works for the International Bird Rescue Research Center. When there's a bad oil spill, people call him and he comes—fast. Thousands of oil-soaked birds will freeze to death or drown unless they can be cleaned off quickly and set free. If they're found quickly enough, washed clean with detergent and released, many birds can be saved.

Jay organizes the volunteers who come to help after a spill and shows them how to handle the birds. He knows. "Even as a kid, I loved animals," he says. "I was always caring for injured sea gulls or turtles. Once I raised a fawn I found in the woods." After high school, he worked for the Marin County Humane Society, where he began learning how to care for wild animals without making them too tame to live wild again. Now he's an expert on wildlife rehabilitation, teaching hundreds of volunteers each year how to save the animals he loves.

Dory Kistner loved playing in the woods near her Long Island home when she was a child and camping out when she was in high school. She liked doing things with her hands—"I work better when I can grab things," she says—and studying marine science in high school. A freshman seminar in the environment at Dartmouth College helped her decide to become an environmental scientist.

Now she does research on the effects of acid rain. Some of her work is in an office, but much of it is outdoors, in the woods. The woods are on Mount Moosilauke, in the White Mountains of New Hampshire, where twenty-seven plots of forest have been precisely

Jay Holcomb.

Dory Kistner-Morris.

surveyed and every tree within them measured. Nearby is a Mountain Cloud Chemistry Project station, where instruments collect meteorological data, ozone concentration data, weekly precipitation samples and hourly rain and cold water samples when the station is in cloud. Readings from this station and from seven smaller stations around the mountain help to explain any changes that occur in the carefully measured trees of the twenty-seven forestry plots.

The data are collected by machine, but a real person has to read them. That's Dory, with another scientist, hiking from one station to another in every kind of weather, all year round.

"It takes good boots," Dory says, "when you're out in minus twenty degree weather!" Good gloves, too—except that you can't screw wires or transfer recorded data to cassette tapes with gloves on, so for several minutes each day her hands have to be bare. But in spite of the cold, this is the kind of hands-on science she loves to do—and she's in the woods she loves.

It is not just the destruction of the rain forests, the acid rain and the ozone layer that should concern us, but also our own communities. . . . It is not all that hard to help in the fight to save our planet, Earth. If we are all a little more caring and careful, we will be much closer to saving our environment for ourselves and for future generations.

—ANDREW HOLLEMAN, 15

Glossary

THE words in this glossary are defined in an environmental context.

adapt To adjust to a new environment or new conditions.

aerate To expose to or supply with air.

algae One- or many-celled plants that contain chlorophyll and live in water.

alternative A possible choice; a different method.

aquatic Living or growing in water.

aquifer Any rock formation that holds or carries water.

available Ready to be used.

biodegradable Capable of decaying and being absorbed by the environment.

biomass The living matter in a specific ecosystem.

canopy The leafy top of forest growth.

contaminate To make unclean or impure.

convert To change to something else.

culture The way of life built up by a group of human beings and passed on from one generation to another.

data A group of facts or information found by measuring or studying a situation.

degradation The wearing down of land by the action of wind, water or erosion.

deplete To decrease or use up.

developed country An industrialized nation where the majority of citizens have a high standard of living. Under 20 percent of the world's population live in these countries.

developing country A poor nation where the majority of citizens do not have a high standard of living.

diversity Variety.

ecology The interrelationship of organisms and their environments.

ecosystem A system formed by the interaction of a community of organisms with their environment.

emission That which is discharged.

emit To discharge or send out.

equator The great circle around the middle of the earth that is equally distant from the North Pole and the South Pole.

fertilizer Substance used to enrich soil.

food chain A series of organisms connected by their feeding habits; each link in the food chain is eaten by a larger one, which is eaten by a still larger one, etc.

fossil fuel Any combustible organic material, like petroleum, coal or natural gas, derived from the remains of prehistoric organisms.

generator A machine that changes one form of energy to another, like heat to electricity.

groundwater Water that has seeped beneath the surface of the ground and is stored in porous rock; the source of springs and wells.

habitat The place where an organism lives and grows naturally.

hydropower Energy derived from the force of moving water.

interdependence When two or more things depend on each other.

irreversible Impossible to change back.

irrigate To supply dry land with water by artificial means.

larva The immature, wingless, feeding stage of many insects.

leaching The passing of liquid through a porous material, like soil.

marine Living in or produced by the sea.

migrate To travel from one place or habitat to another.

native A person, animal or plant of a particular place.

nutrient A nourishing substance.

old-growth forest A mature forest, with many trees that have existed for centuries.

organic Having to do with living things. In farming, growing crops without the use of chemical fertilizers and pesticides.

organism A living thing.

pesticide A chemical preparation for killing pests in homes or on crops.

phosphate A compound of phosphorus that is sometimes found in detergents and fertilizers.

photovoltaic Providing a source of electric current from sunlight.

plankton The mass of tiny floating or drifting organisms in a body of water.

rain forest Dense tropical woodlands.

rehabilitate To bring back to a good condition.

renewable energy Energy that comes from a source that can't be used up, like the sun's heat or the wind.

residue What is left after something is removed, thrown away or used.

resources A supply of environmental benefits, like water or sunlight.

rhizome A horizontal underground stem that puts down roots and sends up shoots.

silt Fine sand or earth carried by moving and running water and settling at the bottom.

solar Of or from the sun.

solvent A substance that can make another substance dissolve.

species A basic group of related individual plants or animals that resemble each other and can reproduce among themselves but not with members of another group.

subspecies A subdivision within a species that differs for geographical or ecological reasons.

sustainable Able to be used in a way that does not deplete; renewable.

toxic Poisonous.

toxin Poison.

transform To change in form, appearance or structure.

turbine A machine driven by blades turned by the force of steam, water, hot gases or air.

urban Having to do with a town or city.

vulnerable Capable of being hurt or damaged.

watershed The region drained by a river or stream.

wetlands Low lands that are periodically or steadily flooded with shallow water.

Reading About the Environment

TODAY there are many books about the environment as a whole, along with books on specific environmental topics like solar energy or hazardous waste. Each season brings new books. You'll find them in bookstores and in libraries. Although some are published for adults and some for children, many books in each category are suitable for both. (For example, although this book is written for kids, it wouldn't hurt an adult to read it.)

At a bookstore, you may find the book you want in a section called The Environment, or Environmental Studies, but you may also find it under Nature or Science. In a library, looking up those topics in the card catalog may lead you to other topics. Whether you're in a library or a bookstore, take time to browse around and see what new books have been published. If you need help to find something, ask for it.

You'll see many interesting articles on the environment in magazines and also in newspapers. Check the TV listings for specials on nature and environmental topics.

Listed below are books and magazines and other materials (in addition to a daily reading of the *New York Times*) that the author of this book found most helpful.

Books

Adopting a Stream: A Northwest Handbook. Steve Yates. Illustrated by Sandra Noel. Seattle and London: An Adopt-a-Stream Foundation Publication distributed by University of Washington Press, 1988. This book clearly explains the relationship of a watershed to the people and wildlife within it.

The Complete Guide to Environmental Careers. CEIP Fund Staff. Covelo, California: Island Press, 1989. Descriptions of real jobs and the people who work at them.

The Greenhouse Trap: What We're Doing to the Atmosphere and How We Can Slow Global Warming. Francesca Lyman and others. Boston: Beacon Press, 1990. Thorough and helpful. Reading list and index.

How to Make the World a Better Place. Jeffrey Hollender. New York: Quill/Morrow, 1990. Suggests what people can learn and do to improve their environment, with a good section on food, hunger and agriculture.

The Poverty of Affluence. Paul Wachtel. Philadelphia: New Society Publishers, 1989. A thoughtful study of what happens to people in developed nations as they become used to an ecologically wasteful way of life.

Save Our Planet. Diane MacEachern. New York: Dell, 1990. Things you can do at home, in the garden, at the supermarket and at school to improve the environment. Lists places to write for information, catalogs and magazines. Gives a clear description of composting. Good resource section and index.

Saving the Earth: A Citizen's Guide to Environmental Action. Will Steger and Jon Bowermaster. Illustrations by Mike Mikos. New York: Knopf, 1990. An excellent overview of environmental problems, with some possible solutions. Includes photographs and diagrams, as well as helpful comic-strip-style explanations that readers are free to reproduce.

State of the World 1990. Lester Brown and others. New York: Norton, 1990. The Worldwatch Institute publishes a yearly report on the world's environment; this volume includes chapters on the advantages of bicycles as transportation, water for agriculture, world hunger and envisioning a sustainable society. Along with other volumes in this series, the essential guide to world-wide environmental problems and creative solutions. With thorough notes and an index.

Magazines

Some single issues of magazines prepared around the time of the twenty-year anniversary of Earth Day present thorough overviews of environmental issues, notably the September 1989 issue of *Scientific American* ("Managing Planet Earth").

Other helpful single issues on the environment include the April/May 1990 issue of *Mother Jones* ("Earth Day 1990"); the May 1990 *Natural History* issue on recycling ("The Endless Cycle"); the special April 1990 issue of *Smithsonian* and the Spring 1990 issue of *Whole Earth Review* ("Helping Nature Heal— Environmental Restoration").

Magazines specifically concerned with the environment include *Audubon; The Nature Conservancy Magazine; E; World-Watch* (the magazine of Worldwatch Institute, which publishes the *State of the World* annuals); *Sanctuary,* published by the Massachusetts Audubon Society; *Garbage* and the kids' magazine *Planet Three.*

Other Helpful Materials

Many environmental-action organizations publish information about their work, among them Educators for Social Responsibility, Greenpeace, and Zero Population Growth. You can find pamphlets from these and other organizations in your library. Information on environmentally sound products can be found in many mail-order catalogs.

Environmental Groups

THERE are hundreds of environmental groups in the United States and Canada and in countries around the world. Some organizations have broad goals, such as protecting wildlife, while others concentrate on very specific goals, like saving whales or whooping cranes. Some groups are national or international and others work in a single town or neighborhood. Some groups emphasize education and others encourage action.

The best place to learn which organizations work on topics that interest you is at your local library.

You'll find descriptions of most groups, along with addresses and phone numbers, in the *Encyclopedia of Associations*. The library is likely to have a file of pamphlets and other materials that are published by environmental organizations to explain their work. It may also subscribe to some environmental magazines in which you will find articles and information about organizations and individuals working for a variety of environmental causes.

Listed here are the names of environmental groups that are mentioned in this book:

BAT CONSERVATION INTERNATIONAL
P.O. Box 162603
Austin, Texas 78746
(512) 327-9721

A group that promotes bat conservation, with an emphasis on education.

CHILDREN'S BEACH HOUSE
1800 Bay Avenue
Lewes, Delaware 19958
(302) 645-9184

A learning center where schoolchildren of Delaware explore their state's shore environment and participate in conservation work.

THE CHILDREN'S RAINFOREST
P.O. Box 936
Lewiston, Maine 04240

An organization that offers children around the world the opportunity to preserve rain forest land in Costa Rica. For information, send a stamped, self-addressed envelope.

CITIZENS CLEARINGHOUSE FOR HAZARDOUS WASTE
P.O. Box 926
Arlington, Virginia 22216
(703) 276-7070

Provides information and assistance to neighborhood groups fighting hazardous waste.

EDUCATORS FOR SOCIAL RESPONSIBILITY
23 Garden Street
Cambridge, Massachusetts 02138
(617) 492-1764

An organization that promotes creative teaching of peace and environmental awareness.

FOOD WORKS
64 Main Street
Montpelier, Vermont 05602
(802) 223-1515

A program that helps students discover the connections between food, farming, hunger and food policy in their own communities and in countries around the world, as they build and maintain school gardens.

GIRL SCOUTS OF THE UNITED STATES
OF AMERICA
830 Third Avenue
New York, New York 10022-7522

GREENPEACE, U.S.A.
1436 U Street N.W.
Washington, D.C. 20009
(202) 462-1177

The U.S. branch of an international organization that works actively for environmental issues.

HABITAT FOR HUMANITY
Habitat and Church Streets
Americus, Georgia 31709-3498
(912) 924-6935

INTERNATIONAL BIRD RESCUE
RESEARCH CENTER
Aquatic Park
Berkeley, California 94710
(414) 841-9086

An organization that studies bird rehabilitation and directs volunteer rescue groups.

KIDS AGAINST POLLUTION (KAP)
Tenakill School
275 High Street
Closter, New Jersey 07624

A network of students working for the environment through letter-writing campaigns and community action.

MASSACHUSETTS AUDUBON SOCIETY
Lincoln, Massachusetts 01773
(617) 259-9500 or (1-800) 541-3443

Works to protect the environment for people and wildlife. An Environmental Helpline provides information and assistance by phone to Massachusetts residents.

NATIONAL AUDUBON SOCIETY
950 Third Avenue
New York, New York 10022
(212) 546-9100

Sponsors a wide variety of programs to preserve plant and animal habitats.

THE NATURE CONSERVANCY
1815 North Lynn Street
Arlington, Virginia 22209
(703) 841-5300

Preserves and protects rare and threatened species in nature sanctuaries in the United States and Latin America.

RENEW AMERICA
1400 Sixteenth Street N.W., Suite 710
Washington, D.C. 20036
(202) 232-2252

A national organization that publishes information on local, state and national environmental programs, including the *Environmental Success Index,* a list of outstanding local programs around the United States.

SEVENTH GENERATION
10 Farrell Street
South Burlington, Vermont 05403
(800) 456-1177

A company that sells environmentally sound products.

STOP WAR TOYS CAMPAIGN
War Resisters League
339 Lafayette Street
New York, New York 10012
(212) 228-0450

TIMBER WOLF ALLIANCE
Sigurd Olson Environmental Institute
Northland College
Ashland, Wisconsin 54806
(715) 682-1223

Works to increase and improve public awareness and acceptance of the wolf in its native habitat and appreciation of its ecological role.

TOXIC AVENGERS
c/o El Puente
211 South Fourth Street
Brooklyn, New York 11211
(718) 387-0404

A group of young people working to prevent the dumping of hazardous waste in their neighborhood.

TREE PEOPLE
12601 Mulholland Drive
Beverly Hills, California 90201
(818) 753-4620

UNITED ANGLERS OF CASA
GRANDE HIGH SCHOOL
Casa Grande High School
333 Casa Grande Road
Petaluma, California 94954
(707) 778-4677

ZERO POPULATION GROWTH
1400 Sixteenth Street N.W., Suite 320
Washington, D.C. 20036
(202) 322-2200

An organization concerned with maintaining a stable balance between the earth's population and its resources.

Canadian Organizations

A selection of Canadian groups with information on saving the environment

CANADIAN ENVIRONMENTAL NETWORK
P.O. Box 1289, Station B
Ottawa, Ontario
K1P 5R3
(613) 563-2078

ECOLOGY ACTION CENTRE
Veith House
3115 Veith Street, 3rd Floor
Halifax, Nova Scotia
B3K 3G9
(902) 454-7828

FRIENDS OF THE EARTH / LES AMIS DE
LA TERRE
251 Laurier Avenue West, Suite 701
Ottawa, Ontario
K1P 9Z9
(613) 230-3352

GREENPEACE FOUNDATION CANADA
578 Bloor Street West
Toronto, Ontario
M6G 1K1
(416) 538-6470

POLLUTION PROBE
12 Madison Avenue
Toronto, Ontario
M5R 2S1
(416) 926-1907

WORLD WILDLIFE FUND
60 St. Clair Avenue East, Suite 201
Toronto, Ontario
M4T 1N5
(416) 923-8173

Index

Photograph Credits

About the Author

Betty Miles's belief that young people want to help preserve the environment inspired her to write the original 1974 edition of *Save the Earth*. She is well known for her many novels, including *All It Takes Is Practice, The Real Me, The Secret Life of the Underwear Champ, Sink or Swim,* and *The Trouble with Thirteen*. She lives in Tappan, New York.